DRAWING
YOUR OWN
CONCLUSIONS

Civil Disobedience Tree

DRAWING YOUR OWN CONCLUSIONS

GRAPHIC STRATEGIES FOR READING, WRITING, AND THINKING

Fran Claggett

with Joan Brown

HEINEMANN
Portsmouth, NH

for Madge Holland
Holden and Phoebe
and
Ron, Jeff, and Lisa Brown

Boynton/Cook Publishers, Inc.
A subsidiary of Reed Elsevier Inc.
361 Hanover Street, Portsmouth, NH 03801–3912

Offices and agents throughout the world

Library of Congress Cataloging-in-Publication Data

Claggett, Fran.
    Drawing your own conclusions : graphic strategies for
reading, writing, and thinking / Fran Claggett with Joan
Brown.
        p.   cm.
    Includes index.
    ISBN 0-86709-293-9
    1. Language arts (Secondary)   2. Literature—Study
and teaching (Secondary)   3. Metaphor.   4. Drawing.
I. Brown, Joan, 1943–   . II. Title.
LB1631.C53   1992
428'.0071'2—dc20   92-28860
                                              CIP

"Lullaby for a Daughter", from *Selected and New Poems
1961–1981* by Jim Harrison. Copyright © 1982 by Jim
Harrison. Used by permission of Delacorte Press/Seymour
Lawrence, a division of Bantam Doubleday Dell Publishing
Group, Inc.

Frontispiece by David Paiva and Doug Alexander.
Back cover photo of Fran Claggett by Madge Holland.
Back cover photo of Joan Brown by Ron Brown.

Designed by Wladislaw Finne.
Printed in the United States of America.
99   5 6 7 8

CONTENTS

ILLUSTRATIONS

PREFACE

To acknowledge the debts one owes in writing a book that makes heavy use of student writing and drawing is to recognize that teaching is essentially a sharing—teacher with teacher, teacher with student, student with student. To acknowledge the origins of ideas and practices is even more difficult. I have tried to indicate germinal sources of our views in the introduction, but here I want to name some names of people who have made direct contributions and also help you sort out the roles that Joan Brown and I each played in the writing of this book.

First, I offer my thanks to Bob Boynton and Peter Stillman for recognizing, in this approach to reading, writing, and thinking through graphics, the need for this book. Peter has been an invaluable critic and editor, and I am grateful for the opportunity to work with him. The special nature of a book that is heavily dependent on student graphics requires the kind of flexibility, problem-solving, and support that Bob, Peter, and the Heinemann staff provide.

I would like to credit James Gray and the Bay Area Writing Project for publishing *Balancing the Hemispheres: Brain Research and the Teaching of English* in 1980. This monograph, with Gabriele Lusser Rico's introduction to clustering, along with a brief but substantive history of brain research up to that time, and my presentation of student work with mandalas and maps, paved the way for *Drawing Your Own Conclusions* ten years later. Although many advances have been made in brain research since that time, the premise of that book still holds: We need to provide specific activities that tap multiple ways of learning in our classrooms.

Working as a teacher/consultant for the Bay Area Writing Project also made possible the contact with the teachers who have contributed their students' work to this book. We would like to acknowledge the contributions from *Piner Poems*, a collection of poetry from Piner High School, Santa Rosa, California, where, from time to time, I have been allowed to be visiting poet and teacher. Our thanks to Richard Lattimore, Brigette Mansell, and other members of the Piner English Department. Other teachers who donated specific student work include Anita Thompson, Assistant Principal from La Serna High School in Whittier, California, and Pat Morrison, formerly from San Ramon High School in San Ramon, California.

Bal Goleman, a former national Teacher of the Year who recently retired from her work as teacher and administrator in Dade County, Florida, experimented widely with the mandala in her work with compensatory education middle school students. Other directors of the University of Miami/Dade County Writing Institute summer program who have contributed significantly include Dr. Eveleen Lorton, Dr. Zelda Glazer, Jenny Krugman, and Dr. Billy Birnie.

Finally, a word about collaboration. You may have noticed that a number of Boynton/Cook books have two authors—testimony to the power of having a writing response partner whether you are student or teacher. While I take responsibility for the Introduction and Afterword, Joan Brown and I share authorship of the bulk of the text. I take primary responsibility for Chapters 1, 3, 5, and the first part of Chapter 6. Joan assumes primary responsibility for Chapters 2, 4, and the latter part of Chapter 6. Chapter 7 is an inextricable amalgamation. As we wrote, we revised each other's work as much as our own, spinning off from each other's ideas in the spirit of writing projects all over the country. It is often difficult for us to remember who wrote the original draft of a particular section.

Selecting the student graphics was a painful process: we began with three times as many as we could use; each paring seemed a great loss to us. We regretted the absence of color and rejected some delicate watercolor graphics, knowing that their effects were too subtle for black and white. For all of the students whose work appears here, there are countless others whose work is equally worthy of publication. Special thanks must go, however, to Mimi Nicosia and Barry Tribuzio, who discovered for themselves the power of the image, both as an end in itself and as a generative source of both prose and poetry. Because of their work, students established the "Fame and Glory" wall in our classroom. The "fame and glory" graphics, providing both challenge and inspiration, raised the aesthetic and analytic level of graphics permanently at our school.

Finally, a note of thanks to our colleagues in the Alameda Unified School District. Teachers from all grade levels have participated over the years in workshops and experiments as we expanded our understanding of how graphics can contribute to reading, writing, and thinking. And a special thanks to Judy Cunningham of Alameda High School; the work of her students alone could have filled the pages of this book.

To all of the contributing teachers and students, we wish to acknowledge our thanks while admitting our continuing wonder at the fecundity of the human mind.

Fran Claggett

DRAWING
YOUR OWN
CONCLUSIONS

The Apple Tree and "Ode on a Grecian Urn"
by Mimi Nicosia

INTRODUCTION

**LOOKING
BACK,
LOOKING
FORWARD**

How it all began: The history

That which is always beginning, over and over

WALLACE STEVENS

The year was so long ago that I don't even like to say it, but I will. It was 1964. The year may be history, but the scene is very contemporary. It could be your classroom. It could be the classroom down the hall. My classroom was large, high-ceilinged, bare-floored. (This was before they built the new, low-ceilinged, carpeted school.) It was filled with old-fashioned desks, the kind I still see in a lot of schools. And it was filled with what were then called Z freshmen. Z as opposed to X. If you were a Z student, you were dumb and you knew it. You went to classes only with other dumb students and you didn't learn much of anything other than how dumb you were. Today we don't have Z students, but we have slow learners, educationally handicapped students, learning-impaired students—special needs students of many designations, including the students who speak from one to five languages other than English.

So I was in this classroom trying to get my Z freshmen to write and they were politely not writing. Suddenly, the door opened and the mechanical drawing teacher, who knew that my room was a collecting place for castoffs of all kinds, including students, came in carrying an armload of long strips of heavy white drawing paper. They were about five inches across and two feet long, obviously scraps left over from a project. "Thought you might be able to use these," he said, waving as he left. Without thinking, I picked up a handful of the strips and went on talking to my kids about writing, then gave them an assignment to write and passed out these odd-shaped strips of paper. Then I sat down at my desk and started preparing for my X's the next period. (I hate to admit things like this, but it's the truth.)

When the bell rang, I looked up, expecting to get maybe one or two pieces of paper back, but the kids were banging their way out of the room already. Then I looked down at the corner of my desk. There was a huge, haphazard stack of these strips, all with writing on them, most of them completely covered, top to bottom, with penciled scrawls.

"Shape," I thought, thinking of all the days before of untouched, lined notebook paper.

The next day, the kids came into the classroom and wanted to know how I liked their writing. I loved it, I told them, and we were going to do some more today, but today, they would be writing in circles. First, however, they had to make the circles out of construction paper. That took a while. Then I gave them crayons and said that before we wrote, we

3

were going to draw. That stopped them. Drawing was for kindergartners. They knew that. Okay, I said, pretend you're kindergartners.

So they pretended, happily regressed to poking each other and not batting an eye when I asked them to think about what animal they were most like and to draw it in their circles. We went on to other questions ("What plant are you like?" "What number are you like?" etc.) and in response, they drew pictures in their circles. When I asked them to write a sentence for each thing they drew, they didn't stop to say, "I can't write." Jennifer said she was like a kitten because she was soft and liked to cuddle and nobody laughed. Sean said he was like a porcupine and nobody better get too close. And Kevin said he was like a zero. He wouldn't say why but in his circle he had written "Zero. The loneliest number in the world."

For me, nothing about that classroom or those kids was ever the same again. They cut out circles and stars and drew and wrote. They made what I came to call *mandalas*, honoring that ancient word for a symbol which integrates aspects of a person or an idea into a circular design. They brought their friends in to see their mandalas on the walls. They read their mandala poetry at "Back to School Night." And my *X* students, those students who had learned to play the game of school, clamored to draw, to make their own mandalas, to begin to think and write beyond the framework of their safe, successful prose.

During the next several years, I continued to expand on the use of graphics in my classroom by trial and error, improvising as the occasion seemed appropriate, adapting assignments from one class to another. Many of my assignments grew off the walls, in a way, as students from one class would get ideas from the drawings and writings that covered nearly everything in the room but the windows. I was beginning to make some connections between the graphics and the chief business of my students—reading, writing, making sense of their reading in terms of their own experiences, making sense of their own experiences. Over the years, as I began to take my ideas into other teachers' classrooms through Bay Area Writing Project workshops and conferences, I gradually came to understand a great deal more about how we think, how we learn, and the role that maps, mandalas, and metaphor play in all of it.

I was extremely fortunate during these developmental years to team teach with Madge Holland, who worked with me to develop specific classroom strategies using what was then very new knowledge in brain research. We saw in that early research a foundation that we had been searching for, some explanations for our understanding of what was working in the classroom. We experimented with heterogeneously grouped humanities courses, balancing what we knew of right hemisphere learning approaches with those of the more traditional left hemisphere. Constant student and teacher self-monitoring of a variety of approaches to literature and writing continued to confirm the importance and power of graphics as part of the balanced curriculum we were attempting to construct.

It has been a long time since 1964, when those first students began to draw mandalas for themselves and for the characters in the books they were reading. Since then we have seen many advances in our understanding of how people learn; we have been part of many changes in how we teach writing and in how we integrate the teaching of literature and writing. Our concept of graphic thinking has expanded significantly and we are still learning.

Why it works: Developing a theoretical base

*Yet to speak of the whole world as metaphor
   Is still to stick to the contents of the mind.*

WALLACE STEVENS

That the use of graphics will help students make meaning as they read, write, and act—the premise of this book—is firmly rooted in current thinking about how the mind works. The burgeoning field of brain research has given rise to multiple theories about how the mind works, how we learn. What they all have in common, however, is the assumption that thinking is an exceedingly complex activity and that there is no single way to teach anything, whether it is reading or throwing a football. Jung has provided many contemporary theorists with organizing principles that fit today's more sophisticated understanding of the brain/mind relationship. I have adapted Jung's concepts of the four primary ways that we make sense out of the world and rephrased his four functions into the terms *observe, analyze, imagine,* and *feel* to describe aspects of a balanced approach to learning.

Most of us learn from using a combination of these approaches, but we find one or two more comfortable, whether from predisposition, habit, or training. Because our schools are set up to teach mainly through analysis, however, by the time students reach the middle and high school years, they've forgotten how to *observe,* don't trust their *feelings,* and sadly relegate their *imaginations* to daydreaming.

It is this lack of balance I have worked to redress. Through the use of graphics, students have opportunities to experience all four functions as they interact with the books they are reading and the essays, stories, and poems they are writing. They learn that thinking is more than analysis (although it involves that, too). And they learn to expand and trust their own ways of knowing in three critical ways:

1. **Making Metaphors:** The most fundamental claim I make for the use of graphics in the classroom is that it teaches students to think metaphorically, the primary way in which we expand our understanding of the world. "Our ordinary conceptual system, in terms of which we both think and act," write Lakoff and Johnson, "is fundamentally metaphorical in nature." Through the use of graphics, students move along the road toward Aristotle's ideal: "The greatest thing by far is to be a master of metaphor."

2. **Making Connections:** Making metaphors is making connections; using graphics helps students make connections between the books

they read and the lives they lead, enabling them to translate their first, formless responses into meaningful words and symbols.

3. **Seeing It Whole:** Much of our time in the English classroom has traditionally been spent in looking at parts of things, as if we were scientists dissecting poems "etherised upon a table." We have, I'm happy to say, come a long way from the dissection model; the use of dialectical journals, calling for students to respond to specific ideas or literary passages with personal anecdotes, feelings, and ideas of their own certainly helps students transact with the text. The graphic element provides another dimension, enabling the student to respond nonverbally, holistically, to the selection. The use of graphics allows students to record their initial, global responses with pictorial maps as well as with words. At the other end of the process, graphics can help students make sense of the parts, thus defying Lewis Carroll and putting Humpty Dumpty together again.

THE GRAPHIC MEMORY

A powerful adjunct to learning that emerged initially as a side benefit from working with graphics is that of both *short- and long-term memory* improvement. Since my teaching relies on students' ability to connect the pieces of literature that they have read throughout the year, I began to notice how the books that students had worked with graphically were the most easily retained. Students frequently referred to their graphic work when discussing, in the spring, a book they had mapped in the fall. They recalled the ideas and issues of the work with rich, specific detail, and talked about the characters as if they had just finished reading the book.

In a more methodical way, I conducted a classroom research study with a group of sophomores who had elected a course entitled "Learning to Learn." Students were willing subjects as we experimented with various learning styles. In one experiment, we tried a number of different ways of learning vocabulary: auditory, visual, kinesthetic; contextual and non-contextual; and graphic. In the graphic study, students drew pictures to help them recall the meaning of each word for the week. We did weekly, monthly, and semester testing, not for grades, but for student understanding of their own optimal learning strategies. Although students demonstrated some retention of their understanding of words by all of the methods, they dramatically improved their retention of the words for which they had drawn pictures.

GRAPHICS AND AT-RISK STUDENTS

All students are at risk, in my opinion, but there are particular groups of students who have very special needs that can be addressed by involving them in metaphoric thinking and drawing:

1. Students who are new to this country and just learning its language as well as its customs may find their way to language through pictures. Many cultures value imagistic thinking much more highly than they do

analytical thinking. Watching these students blossom when encouraged to use their natural modes of expression is one of the joys of being in the classroom.

2. Students who, diagnosed as "learning disabled," may indeed be able to learn when given a chance to try other ways of learning. These students may be encouraged to act or draw; I have presented the graphics work to many groups of Special Education teachers and have seen the mandalas and maps their students have produced. I cannot recount the number of times I have heard the statement, "The mandala-generated sentences are the first thing this student has written in my class."

3. The culturally "deprived" students—deprived of the dominant culture of the schoolroom, but perhaps rich in their own subculture—respond to the opportunity to draw from their own environment. Because the act of drawing metaphorically taps archetypal imagery, these students begin to make connections, to see themselves as possessing a wealth of knowledge they didn't know they had. Working on group projects that involve the physical act of making something frees these students from the school syndrome of failure that many have grown used to. The step to writing becomes smaller.

4. The academically "gifted," who either drop out from boredom or learn to play the game of school effectively, make straight A's, and compete for scholarships to the best universities, may be reluctant at first to engage in such kindergarten activities as drawing. Many of these students have never had an art or music course; the drive to academic excellence tragically prevents them from the very activities that would tap the essence of being an educated person. Once captivated by the challenge, however, these students quickly lose their fear of the unknown. Searching for appropriate metaphors and symbols, they begin to interact with texts and with other students in deeply extended discussions about character motivation, author intention, diction, structure—the very things that we used to have to guide them toward in lectures or teacher directed assignments.

There are unlimited ways of dividing up the at-risk students; there are unlimited ways of reaching these students, but most of them take time, money, small classes, special training. What we offer in this book is just one additional approach for you to integrate into your classroom, one way of empowering all of these students to use their minds, feelings, and eyes. By gaining consciousness of how they learn, they gain some control of their own lives.

The claims that we make for the power of using graphics to develop metaphoric thinking and improve memory are *authoritative* in the basic sense of *having the sanction or weight of authority; substantiated or supported by documentary evidence*. In this case, the authority comes from twenty-five years of work with graphics in the classroom and is supported not only by psychologists and brain researchers, but by anecdotal evidence from hundreds of teachers throughout the country who have used these assignments.

The networking community

When I began to think seriously of making a book out of all of the ideas and materials I had been sharing with teachers through the years, I turned to a colleague, Joan Brown, who had joined our department in 1980. Joan had been developing her own strategies in visual thinking and brought with her a creative energy that resulted in exciting new ways of using metaphoric and visual thinking. She, too, began to accumulate portfolios of graphic maps, along with transcripts of student presentations which were invaluable in letting us see exactly how students process information about their own learning. It was my good fortune that Joan agreed to work with me in what has truly become a joint undertaking.

Other teachers, especially those I met through my work with the Bay Area and National Writing Projects, have been invaluable in building up our classroom base of understanding how the mind works in the interplay among student, text, and teacher. Valuable corroboration for our specific work in metaphorical thinking has come from many other sources, as well. Some works that have been useful in helping us talk about our own thinking include James Moffett's work with the universe of discourse; James Britton's seminal work on writing process; Janet Emig's discussion of the interrelationship among the hand, eye, and brain; Ann Berthoff's always provocative theories about thinking and writing; Lauren Resnick's definition of how to know when thinking is going on; Gabriele Rico's applications of the recent advances in brain research to writing; Howard Gardner's theories of the intellect; George Lakoff and Mark Johnson's work on the role of metaphor in thinking; and the resurgence of professional interest in Louise Rosenblatt's transactional approach to literature. In addition, the words of scientists, writers, and mathematicians, as they describe their own creative processes, give our work with graphics a solid validity. Einstein's account of his own creative process stands as an example:

The psychical entities which seem to serve as elements of thought are certain signs and more or less clear images which can be "voluntarily" reproduced and combined. . . . this combinatory play seems to be the essential feature in productive thought—before there is any connection with logical construction in words or other kinds of signs which can be communicated to others.

An invitation

This book is set up to be a practical guide on how to help kids read, write, and think through the use of graphic maps and mandalas. The concepts that support the assignments are appropriate for all students at all levels, kindergarten through college, Advanced Placement to Learning Disabled. While there are many specific suggestions for classroom assignments, most of you will quickly spin off ideas to fit your students, your curriculum, your style of teaching. One of the exciting parts of taking my work with graphics to teachers all over the country is seeing how teachers pick up an idea such as the Sun-Shadow Mandala and make something of their own with it, something that fits into their personal framework of teaching.

We are always searching to find ways of translating what we know into how we teach. It's my belief and my hope that you will find a new slant on how best to teach reading, writing, and thinking, or perhaps, some corroboration and elaboration of what you are already doing. We as teachers need to assume and share the authority that comes from our experience, and that is what this book is about.

FRAN CLAGGETT

Personal Mandala by Judi Rich

PART ONE

THE FOUNDATIONS OF GRAPHIC THINKING

Learning—whatever else it might be—is surely a disposition to form structures.

GORDON ALLPORT

Using graphics to learn certainly isn't new. Long before the invention of the alphabet, people depicted events in their lives on cave walls; we believe that they used pictographs to convey messages. Today we are bombarded by graphics—not only in the most obvious ways, such as media advertising, but also in every aspect of business and industry. Just browsing in any airport sundries shop reveals at least a dozen different computer magazines, each one about eighty percent composed (literally) of computerized graphics using color, design, words, and symbols. The lead article in one recent computer magazine, written by a major industry's CEO, challenged our schools to teach students how to survive in today's world—by learning to think graphically.

A child's first book is pictures, the words coming later. We know that children learn to create and "read" pictures long before they learn to read words, relying first on graphic images to convey meaning. The sequence naturally follows the "ontogeny recapitulates phylogeny" model that our study of language and literature embraces.

What are we to make of our knowledge about the origins of language, the pictograph on the cave wall and the picture book in the nursery? What are we to make of the explosion of computer graphics? What does it all have to do with reading a novel or writing a poem?

In this book we offer a tentative explanation that may at first look and sound too simple to be valid, but that may help link the traditional language of learning—the word—with the original language of communication—the symbol. The link is metaphor. Through it, we make the connections between experience and history. "Metaphor," as Lakoff and Johnson have so succinctly stated, "is not merely a matter of language. It is a matter of conceptual structure. And conceptual structure is not merely a matter of the intellect—it involves all the natural dimensions of our experience, including aspects of our sense experiences: color, shape, texture, sound."

Our primary goal as teachers is to enable students to explore, through the dimensions of the senses, the power of the mind; to provide situations in which they can engage in all of the four functions—observing, analyzing, imagining, feeling; to help them gain the confidence to recognize and claim their creations and responses; and to provide them with the tools that will enable them to go back to the text—a poem, a film, a witnessed action—to validate and prove their ideas.

Through studying a novel, for example—observing the characters and feeling their emotions; imagining the framework of time and space; analyzing the structure and style—students discover the connections between themselves and the novelist's fictional world. Northrop Frye urges us to "make what we read part of our own vision, and understand something of its function in shaping that vision." The student's increasingly conscious ability to make connections between the world of literature and the world of everyday reality brings with it a growing awareness and understanding of the work itself, and of the way in which that work gives shape to human experience.

The graphic process that we detail in this book empowers students to take charge of their own learning. Through making connections graphically, students can explore the relationships and interactions of literature (character, style, structure) and of life (people, culture, science, government). Making mandalas encourages students to see connections between their subjects (themselves, a character, an idea) and symbolic archetypes. They gain insight into the subject they are addressing and how that subject fits into the world. Through the mapping process, students begin to understand interrelationships between the parts and the whole. As they map ideas, they are thinking in a non-linear, holistic way, graphically interweaving symbols and words to make meaning of their experiences. It is this symbolic process of integrating the hand, the mind, and the eye that permits the kind of linear articulation that you'll find in Part II as students explain, invent, and argue for their insights.

Through the graphic processes that we offer in this book, students are engaged in both abstract and visual as well as specific and analytical thinking. They move from visual to verbal thinking and back again, learning how to use each of these thinking dimensions to discover, develop, and substantiate their own ideas and perceptions.

It is critical for us as teachers to address the need for all students to be able to communicate both visually and verbally, integrating one into the other, so that they can participate in the symbolic experiences that make us most wholly human.

CHAPTER 1

THE MANDALA: THE WORD AND THE SYMBOL

The concept of *mandala*, as we use it in this book, is drawn from the ancient idea of the circular shape as an archetype denoting the integration of a number of elements to make a whole. Drawing a mandala in its simplest form, a circle with an uncomplicated design in it, is a natural precursor to writing; the symbol of the mandala appears universally in the earliest scribbles of children and on the cave walls of prehistoric peoples. It forms a dominant motif in the mature art of every culture, as well, from the Rose Windows in great Christian cathedrals to the sand paintings of the Navaho to the intricate mandalas of India, China, and Japan.

Rhoda Kellogg, teacher and author of *The Psychology of Children's Art*, has exhibited an impressive collection of mandalas drawn by preschool children from eighteen countries. Regardless of language or culture, all children demonstrate a mandala-drawing phase, often just a circle around intersecting vertical and horizontal lines. Kellogg found a strong correlation between early reading and writing success and the rich pre-school experiences in art which allowed the children to move through the natural stages of drawing.

The sun-shadow mandala

The Sun-Shadow Mandala assignment involves students in working with dualities found within themselves, others, literary characters, character relationships or concepts. The process of making a mandala moves from making metaphors (using the functions of *imagine* and *feel*), to choosing specific attributes for each metaphor (using the functions of *observe* and *analyze*), to integrating them into a circular design. The student uses all four functions in the process of planning, drawing the mandala, and weaving both the sun and shadow metaphors into sentences which frame the drawing.

The writing that follows mandala construction ranges from simple poems to complex studies of character, style, and idea. In the balanced curriculum that includes all four functions—observe, analyze, imagine, and feel—students experience a wide variety of writing types ranging from the poetic and reflective to interpretive and evaluative. Whatever the specific writing assignment, students learn to develop and expand their control of language as they play with and fine tune their natural metaphor-making talents.

The use of the terms *sun* and *shadow* in this particular assignment is consistent with an archetypal approach to metaphor. Students select their sun images by thinking analytically, considering alternatives; they are using the "sun side" or Apollonian aspect of their minds. They select shadow images by moving through a process of word choices, arriving at their images by opposition; they are using the "shadow side" of their minds, more clearly associated with mythology of the moon.

The concept of sun-shadow images arises from considering the place of dualities in literature and in our lives. Although it may seem superficial to think in terms of dualities, our history is filled with philosophies that are built on concepts of opposites. (Charles Hampden-Turner's *Maps of the Mind* is a useful, graphically depicted history of the philosophies of dualities throughout history.) It is important to acknowledge that things are never as simple as good and evil, war and peace, inner and outer, the haves and the have nots. Being aware of dualities, however, is a helpful starting point for understanding the more subtle complexities of personality and character motivation.

INSTRUCTIONS FOR THE SUN-SHADOW MANDALA

1. Selecting the sun images

Frost's often-quoted remark that "poetry is talking about one thing in terms of another" provides a useful way of introducing students to the idea of thinking of one thing in terms of another. As students experience using metaphor to understand characters or ideas, they are led to explore the intricate role that metaphor plays in thinking itself.

To begin the Sun-Shadow Mandala assignment for the first time, ask students to move into a quiet, receptive frame of mind, and write down their responses to the following questions. Tell them that there is no discussion at this point, but they will have lots of opportunities to talk later.

The first question is

1. "What animal are you most like?"

Give students a moment or two, not too long, then go on.

2. "What plant are you most like?"

Continue, without discussion, asking for responses to each of the following categories:

3. What color are you most like?
4. What shape are you most like?
5. What number are you most like?
6. What mineral or gem are you most like?
7. What natural element are you most like: air, earth, fire, or water?

Note: For the element, they may choose some aspect of the element or the entire category: *breeze*, *hurricane*, or *tornado* for *air*, for example; or *mountain*, *desert*, or *beach* for *earth*).

These seven symbols become the *sun images* for their mandalas. The concept of *sun image* arises naturally from the method of arriving at these images in a thoughtful, conscious manner, in "the light of day" as we say.

To bypass the language barrier, students may sketch their ideas directly on the chart. (See Figure 1–1.)[1] Later, students work together to provide

[1] All figures are located at the end of each chapter.

the less language-proficient students with the words they need. With some groups, especially with young children or with students whose native language is not English, it may be useful to do some brainstorming or clustering about specific categories before beginning this exercise. Elementary and Special Education teachers say that they often spend a class period for each of the categories, using such questions as these:

PLANT

Are you a tree, a shrub, a flower, a weed?
Are you indoor or outdoor? Wild or domesticated?
Are you evergreen or deciduous?
Are you deeply rooted?
Do you require a great deal of care? of food? of water?

SHAPE

Are you angular or curved?
Are you closed or open?
Are you regular or erratic?
Are you finite or infinite?

NUMBER

Are you even or odd?
Are you whole or a part?
What is your shape? smooth and flowing or pointed and angular?
Are you a single digit? double?

After students have completed their list of sun images, I ask them to go over it with a classmate, checking for specificity: *cat*, for example, is too general; they might choose *Siamese* or *lion* or *white tiger* instead, and search for a trait that typifies that particular kind of cat.

2. Writing the sun sentences

The next step is to write a sentence for each of their specific symbols. Students may use the following core sentence as they think through their primary reason for selecting each of their sun images. There may be a number of reasons why a student selects a giraffe, for example; but in this part of the exercise, you ask for a specific choice and ask them to think about the single most important characteristic that they share with the giraffe.

Suggested core sentence:

I am like the (sun image) because, like the (item), I _____.

Student Examples:

I am most like poison oak because, like poison oak, I am harmless until I'm stepped on.

I am most like a giraffe because, like the giraffe, my vision extends beyond my reach.

If students are having difficulties, have them cluster characteristics on the chalkboard as a class or work in small groups.

3. Selecting sun image qualities

After students have generated their sun images and the seven sentences elaborating on the nature of their relationships, pass out the mandala chart (see Figure 1–1) or have students construct one from a model on the board. Ask them to fill in column 1, the *sun images*. To fill out column 2, students will need to find one word to express *the single characteristic or quality* that represents the underlying reason for each choice and place that "quality" word in column two on the chart. Selecting these words is not easy; it can be a rigorous vocabulary activity. We emphasize to our students that selecting these words is a key activity. Even if they end up with a word they first thought of, they use this word with a firm knowledge of its appropriateness. We encourage students to use the dictionary, the thesaurus, the library, and each other during this part of the process. We also encourage a lot of talk at this point as students help each other select words with the right nuances or connotations. It is extremely important, however, for each student to assume authority for the words he or she chooses. Students might discover that although two or three of them have selected the same animal, their reasons for that selection are very different. One student may be most like a lion because of its strength, another because of its voraciousness.

4. Selecting the shadow images

After column two is filled out, they are ready to move to the idea of opposites, or the *shadow images*. We ask students to move from the outward, or sun images, to the inward aspects of their lives and generate a shadow image for each of the seven categories that will make up the mandala.

Looking at the quality they have ascribed to their animal image, and using the thesaurus as a guide, they should fill in the first line, column three, with an antonym for that word. Have them check to see that the word they choose is the same part of speech. For example, if their sun quality is *intense*, for the panther, their shadow quality might be *lethargic* rather than *lethargy*. In column four, they write the name of the most *lethargic* animal they can think of, such as *cow*. We always work through a few of these together as a class before they begin to work individually on their shadow images. (See Figure 1–2 for an example of a completed chart.)

5. Writing shadow sentences

You may at this point or later, when students are working with their writing, have them write shadow sentences, using some form of core sentence, such as "Inwardly, I am like a _____ because _____." We recommend using these sentences with ESL students: the practice of following a loose sentence model while writing their own ideas is helpful.

6. Drawing the sun-shadow mandala

The directions for actually drawing the mandala are very simple:

> Within the framework of a circle, using color and shape, but no words, draw or symbolize all of your sun images and all of your shadow images. Arrange them in any way that you like. You may want to consider how you place things in relation to each other or you may want to consider only the way the colors and shapes look together.

It's important to stress the idea that the artistry of the drawing isn't important. Encourage students to use symbols if they can't draw something they have selected. For example, a simple drawing of the footprint of a bear can stand for a bear. They can discuss with each other ideas for how to symbolize something they cannot draw.

The act of drawing the symbols is an important step in the process; actually drawing the mandala requires the student to consider relationships among the symbols (depicted by size, color, placement, interaction), deepening insights into character. The completed Sun-Shadow Mandala, in which the student explores both the outward (sun) and the inward (shadow) aspects of personality, presents a visual portrayal of character that translates easily and naturally into writing.

7. Framing the mandala: Writing the sun-shadow sentences

When most students have finished the drawing (from one to three class periods, depending on the students) give them the instructions for the sentences they will write around their mandalas, providing a frame for the drawing:[2]

> Write a single sentence using all of your sun signs. See how you can weave all of these images together in one sentence. Then weave your seven shadow signs into a sentence. Write both of these sentences around the outside of your mandala.

[2]Some teachers have experimented with having students write their framing sentences before they begin to draw. They report that when students write the sentences first, the drawings tend to be merely illustrative. Having students *draw before they write results in much more evocative mandalas.*

8. The completed sun-shadow mandala

Figures 1–3, 1–4, and 1–5 show a variety of approaches to the personal Sun-Shadow Mandala. Some students use the sun and shadow animals as dominant integrating forces while others give equal weight to all the elements. Some students indicate clear distinctions between the sun and shadow sides; others have integrated the elements throughout the drawing. Some students integrate their sun and shadow images into complete scenes, while others keep all elements disparate but integrate the whole through the use of design or color. (Although the illustrations are reproduced in black and white, the original mandalas rely heavily on the use of color.)

9. Sharing through talk

Talk is a vital aspect of all the graphic work we do in our classrooms. We are learning more and more forcefully every year how important talk is to learning. As students share their mandalas, talk about their reasons for selecting specific images, and read their sun-shadow sentences aloud, they frequently come to new understandings. Talking can be done in small groups or with the entire class; we encourage students to be alert to fresh insights and to remember to write about these in their ongoing process logs, a record of their ideas and responses, as we move through the school year.

10. The mandala wall

Once the mandalas are completed, students put them up on the walls of the classroom. Students may be reluctant at first, but we make no exceptions—all mandalas go up and all mandalas have names on the front. This serves two purposes: educationally, students take responsibility for their own achievement; and, logistically, we can quickly record their participation. (More on how we assess graphics in Part III.)

The mandalas create a dramatic display. If your first mandala assignment has been for students to create a personal mandala, the wall creates a portrait of the entire class. If the mandalas have been literary, exploring the characters of a work under study, you have an immediate insight into how students perceive these characters. In high schools, where students move every period, the mandalas create a lot of good cross-talk among students from different classes, often accompanied by "When are we going to get to draw?"

From the mandala to writing

The mandala leads easily and naturally into a variety of extended writing activities, from poems to interpretive character studies to reflective or analytic papers on concepts common to a number of literary works. In this chapter, we include examples of poems that have come from the personal sun-shadow mandala. Additional writing assignments will be illustrated in Parts II and III; for examples of writing emerging from the literary mandala, see Chapter 6, "The Literary Mandala."

POEMS FROM PERSONAL MANDALAS

Poems stemming from mandala work take many forms. Some arise directly from the sun-shadow framing sentences; others elaborate on a single sun or shadow element. One format that students like very much is loosely based on "Winter," a published student poem written by Tom Richards.[3] Using the opening line as a model, students focus on one of their sun-shadow mandala elements, elaborating their original sentences into full poems. Here is Richards' poem, followed by student models:

WINTER

If he were
a season
he'd be Winter.
Not one of these

winters which scream in
but a sly one that caught
you by
surprise, like the
clap of thunder that
comes just after
lightning has hit.
He'd be

the leader of
all seasons in
his own flawless way,
but not good for others.

With his blue icy tones, he'd
watch out for hot weather
standing up to it
from far away

but when it got too close
he'd creep out
just as he'd come.

                    TOM RICHARDS

---

[3] The poem "Winter," which appears in Florence Grossman's book *Getting from Here to There*, (Boynton/Cook, 1982) was itself modeled after George MacBeth's poem "Marshall."

FALL

If I were a season
I'd be fall—
Not a dreary fall
one that is dull,
But a bright and
colorful fall,
full of fiery reds,
sunshine-bright yellows,
and pumpkinny oranges.
With my bright colors
I'd cheer even the saddest
of people.
Raking leaves would be an experience
of utter compulsion—
to be near the smell and feeling
in the wind
Would be like the feeling
you have when you're in love.

                              YVONNE RODRIGUEZ

RED

If I were a color I'd be red.
Not a timid light rosy red,
but a bright plump cherry red.

I'd shimmer my color through
candied apples, pleasant
pomegranates, and meaty melons.

I'd be the color of life,
The color of blood that courses
through the thin veins of every
animal, even man.

I'd be an important color,
An indispensable color,
A triumphant, vivid red.

                        CHARISSE CHISOLM

The next poem shows an elaborated metaphor that, although it begins the
same way as the two previous poems, arose spontaneously from the
student's work with the mandala images.

If I were a stream
I would flow beyond
the edges of the world.
My white foam
would make its home
along my grass-lined banks.

No land would be foreign
because I hold a special
power no stationary
lake can hold.

I am free to flow through
the hearts of many,
pushing about the weaknesses
of others who
have no defense of their own.

DORMI CIMINO

It is unusual to find a student who selects the geometric element, as Susi
does in this extract:

If I could be
anything,
I would be
a line.

Not a ray
or a segment,
but a line
that goes on forever.

A line
in either direction,
the queen of
radii and chords.
A line
that has no shape
and no confinement.

A line
with many points
to mark my feelings.
A line
I could look down
and see no end.

A line
that would not
die.

SUSI ANDERSON

Some poems arise directly out of the integrating sun or shadow sentence
that framed the mandala, as in this example.

The obsidian
Black wolf
Stalked untamed
Through the cold
Snow under the shadow
Of an oak tree
Towards the square
Log cabin.

JOE NEVES

These poems were all written by students during a single class period
following their first experience with the sun-shadow mandala. Students
often follow up their in-class writing with a sequence of poems, focusing
on a number of their symbols.

SUN-SHADOW HAIKU

The haiku, a highly condensed, three-line Japanese poetic form, is
particularly well-suited to the sun-shadow design. Each pair of images
from a mandala can be elaborated into a single haiku. We often assign
one or two haiku, giving students the option of writing an entire haiku
sequence using five to seven of the sun-shadow categories. Writing a sun-
shadow haiku series helps students understand the nature of the haiku,
which usually incorporates contrasting images from nature into a strict
three-line poem. The result is a kind of counterpoint that allows the reader
to infer the connection between the images. Even though many
contemporary American or English haiku do not observe the syllable
count, we prefer to hold to it in this exercise as a way of forcing the
interplay between form and meaning, letting each influence the other. This
practice makes a useful touchstone for extended literary analysis later
when we are reading more complex works. With younger students,
however, or with students who have difficulties with language, we often
use words rather than syllables as our count.

EXAMPLE OF HAIKU WRITING PROCESS

Working first with an entire class to demonstrate the process, we begin by
asking for a sentence that makes a statement about one of their sun
animals. Length of line is not important.

Example:

The exhausted butterfly flew over the water searching for land.

Then we ask for sentences for the shadow animal, a whale, and choose this one:

The whale rose to the surface of the water and lingered there, an island.

At this point we introduce the form of the haiku: three lines, with 5, 7, 5 syllables respectively. We now begin to work to restructure our images into that form. Our next version reads:

The butterfly, off course over water,	10 syllables
landed on an island.	6 syllables
Accommodating whale.	6 syllables

We try again, searching now for words that will fit the haiku form:

Butterfly, damp wings,	5 syllables
Rests on the whale's back.	5 syllables
Migrating island.	5 syllables

Closer! The next try results in this haiku, which satisfies us:

Wing-damp butterfly
Rests to dry on the whale's back.
Migrating island!

Here are three examples of additional sun-shadow haiku:

Great blue heron, why
Do you stand so, head tucked? Does
The bee sting you, too?

The thistle displays
Its weapons like a peacock.
O deceptive rose!

Seven pelicans
Triangulate the heavens—
One vanishing dot!

When introducing haiku for the first time, we work first with a class haiku, letting it take shape on the board or screen. When we reach a point where the class version is close but not yet complete, or when students are calling out so many possibilities, we stop all discussion and have each student or pair of students construct a final version. When we compare, we find that students have discovered many successful options. They are then ready to begin working on their individual sequence.

ADDITIONAL WRITING SUGGESTIONS: PAGES OF POSSIBILITIES

Mandala poems come naturally and easily from the personal sun-shadow mandala exercise; many of them turn up in the submissions to the literary magazine each year. But we don't want to lose sight of our long-term goal, which is to make the process of metaphoric thinking as inherent and free-flowing as these poems. Students who experience a curriculum balanced to include all four functions—observe, analyze, imagine, and feel—use imagery and metaphor in their writing whether they are writing poems or studies of character, style, and idea: Whatever the specific writing assignment, students learn to develop and expand their control of language as they play with and fine tune their natural metaphor-making talents. Here are some suggestions for additional writing possibilities:

1. Write a poem about the subject of your mandala (yourself or a character from literature), using the sun/shadow images as a base.
2. Choose one of your sun/shadow images. Write an extended metaphor, drawing on more characteristics of that image to build a poem or prose piece.
3. Using one set of your sun/shadow sentences, work the ideas into a haiku. In the process of transforming two ideas into three lines with 5, 7, and 5 syllables each, experiment with deleting words, finding alternatives, adding and subtracting until you're happy with the result, which will often be completely unlike the two original sentences.
4. Write a reflective essay, using one of the sun/shadow images as a base. You might explore, for example, how a particular image works throughout a life or a novel.
5. Write an interpretive essay exploring the way a character from literature changes in the course of the work. Use several of your sun or shadow images.
6. Write an autobiographical incident about a time when you behaved like your sun animal.
7. Imagine a situation in which your "animal" sign (sun or shadow) would really show. Under what conditions are you most dominated by your shadow images? by your sun images?

Variations on a theme

As individuals go through a rudimentary mandala drawing stage very early, it is sometimes useful to begin with very simple mandala exercises when working with special education classes. We have worked with special education teachers to design a number of mandala exercises that are especially adapted to high school students with particular needs. For students who have been unsuccessful in learning through traditional methods, the mandala can provide access to language through image. These very basic, simple versions of mandala work incorporate our basic goal in language instruction—to stimulate and structure patterns of the metaphoric and symbolic thinking that underlie all aspects of language use.

BASIC MANDALAS

1. The dream mandala

Some teachers use the dream mandala as a way of beginning the day with very young, even pre-school children. Children come to school fresh from their dreams, often vivid, fascinating half-formed recollections. The dream mandala gives validation to a part of their lives that is often neglected. Older students and adults often find that drawing as well as writing out their dreams provides rich raw material for poetry, journal, or fiction.

For middle and high school students, the dream mandala may form a separate journal section or be incorporated into a regular journal. Students draw images recalled from a dream, using the circular form of the mandala to frame the symbols. After drawing, they write whatever the images of the dream-drawing suggest. During journal sharing, students often read from the mandala writing that has become a regular part of the journal process.

2. The place mandala

The *place mandala* would be appropriate if you wanted to introduce the importance of *place* in a story you were reading with the class or if you were going to have students write about the importance of a particular place in their lives. Teachers find that it works especially well to focus on some very specific aspect of place—a place where you feel peaceful, or happy, or lonely, or frightened. If you're tying it to literature, your choice will be determined by the importance of the place in the story. You could do a number of different place mandalas for a kind of visual journal, each one followed by the student's verbal description and explanation, either oral or written.

Instructions:

1. Draw a circle.
2. Think of a place where you feel peaceful (for example). Inside the circle draw a picture of yourself.
3. Inside the circle put all the things that make you feel peaceful in that place.
4. Title your mandala with your name for the place or for your feeling about the place.

Instructions for a literary place mandala would simply substitute a character from the story for the self. The titling of the mandala is important as it helps bring focus to the entire process.

3. The shape mandala

The final assignment in this section is especially good for giving focus to a field trip to a science or art museum; it may also be used to introduce students to the prevalence of particular shapes in the environment or culture of a group of people. Clustering the circular shape of the mandala, for example, led one group to come up with these examples:

- the galaxy
- the sun
- a snowflake
- Yeats' Great Wheel
- a daisy
- the eye
- the Medicine Wheel
- the color wheel
- Stonehenge
- Mandala
- Navajo sand paintings
- a cut kiwi fruit
- the Rose Windo
- a wedding ring
- the Aztec Calendar
- a child's drawing of a face
- quilt patterns

Instructions for the shape (circle) mandala

Cut out a large circle from a piece of construction paper and use it for making notes as you walk around the museum (or carry on research in the library). Draw and label all of the circles you find.

For the Mandala: Draw a large circle. Inside, draw all examples you found during your study. If you're looking for circles in the classroom, for example, you might draw the hole in the pencil sharpener, the clock, the takeup reel of a projector, someone's buttons, everyone's eyes, the doorknob. A science field trip might lead you to circles of trees, flowers, and stones, as well as circles of animal shapes.

Shift to Writing: Write a poem about circles, using images from your mandala. Write a line or two for every example you found. Just describe it as it looked to you, including things like size, color, number.

You might have students work in groups to compose group or class poems, calendars or collections of mandalas, each person selecting a favorite circular shape, drawing it, and writing a line or two to describe it. The collection could be bound and given to a nearby convalescent hospital or other group of people who might enjoy the student art work and writing.

This activity can be extended beyond the circular shape of the mandala to the basic shapes often used to signify the four elements that the ancients believed made up our universe: the *circle* represented *air*; the *square, earth*; the *triangle, fire*; and the *crescent, water*. In working with students on a museum or science field trip, you can give out all four shapes at random, one to each student. They then look for and record everything they find in that particular shape, proceeding as with the circle exercise.

Visualization and the sun-shadow mandala

One of the problems that many people have in reading is being unable to visualize what they read. When we stop an oral reading of a play, for instance, the most visual kind of writing, and ask students to draw what is going on, they're frequently unable to. It isn't that they can't visualize; they simply are out of the habit of visualizing as they read. Thinking involves seeing, and we have found that listening with an eye toward drawing keeps students' visualizing ability from atrophy.

It may take a little time for students to learn to sit quietly, backs straight but relaxed, eyes closed. We suggest warm-up exercises for several days before you begin an extended visualization.

Warm-ups can be very simple. Begin by having students close their eyes, sit up straight but relaxed, and be quiet. They will have a chance to talk and share their mental pictures later.

1. *Color:* Have students *think a color*. This exercise takes just a minute or two and helps prepare them for longer exercises. Choose a color to match the mood of the day or to change it. If the students come into the class excited from lunch and you want them to be quiet for a reading period, for example, have them begin by thinking *red*, a very active color, then move to *blue*, a quieter color.
2. *Numbers:* If you're introducing the concept of numbers as archetypes or symbols, have them visualize numbers one through ten, very slowly. When they open their eyes, have them draw the numbers the way they saw them in their minds. Some will draw very elaborate numbers, some very simple. They can talk about why they drew them the way they did and what different numbers mean to them.
3. *Shapes:* By asking students to visualize different shapes or scenes, you can lead them into a particular contextual setting for a story or poem. Imagining a scene from a novel or play before they read it results in a variation of Edmund Wilson's "shock of recognition" and heightens student readiness for the work.

These warmup exercises underscore the assumption that the teacher acknowledges and values different ways of seeing. They also train students to become active listeners, which has direct carryover into becoming active readers, as well.

PRE-MANDALA EXTENDED VISUALIZATION EXERCISE

The first extended visualization exercise, while it may be used as an end in itself, works well to introduce special education students to the more complex version of the sun-shadow mandala.

Preparation: Have students sit up straight, but relaxed, with their eyes closed. Have paper and crayons or markers on the desks.

Read slowly to the class, pausing at the / marks.

> Today you are going to take a journey into your mind. For this journey, I want you to pretend to be an animal. Think about how you feel and act when you're very happy. What animal seems most like you when you're feeling happy? Remember that animals can be anything from birds to monkeys to bears, from whales to fish to insects, from cats to rabbits to dogs. / Have you thought of an animal? / Picture this animal clearly in your mind. / Notice its color. If you want to, you can change its color. You can make it any color you want. Decide what color your animal will be. Remember that this animal is like you when you are happy. / Now pretend to be this animal and see how it feels. Have your animal doing something that it likes to do. What is your animal doing now? / You, as your animal, are now going to have an adventure. You're going to meet another animal on your adventure. You are going to meet an animal that is like another part of you. You're going to meet an animal that is like you when you are sad. What is this animal? / Remember that this animal can be any animal at all. Where is this animal? / What is it doing? / Now for the adventure: Your happy animal is going to meet up with your sad animal and try to make it happy, too. Think of how you can have your happy animal meet your sad animal. / Are you ready? / Now let your mind make up the story of how the happy animal meets the sad animal and makes it happy. / When you reach the end of your story, draw your story in the circle on your desk.

Give time for the mental adventure. As students begin to draw, walk around the room and let them tell you what they are drawing. When the students have finished their drawings, they should have a chance to share either with the whole class or with a small group. During this process, other students should be encouraged to ask questions probing for more details. Encourage students to play with their understanding of reality. You want them to be free to let a monkey meet a butterfly, a whale meet a kitten.

After the sharing time, ask students to write the stories they have just shared. As they write, they may make any changes they wish. Encourage the sense of control over their own stories. They are the authors, the final arbiters of all choices.

After students have had the experience of an extended visualization, they may be ready for the full version of the Sun-Shadow Mandala as described earlier. Those of you who work with younger students or with the developmentally disabled, however, may wish to use this simpler

version of the Sun-Shadow Mandala which incorporates the animal
visualization just described.

THE HAPPY-SAD MANDALA: A SIMPLER VERSION
OF THE SUN-SHADOW MANDALA

Remind students of the animals they chose to represent themselves when
they are happy and when they are sad. Ask them whether they would
choose the same animal today to represent them when they are happy. If
not, what animal would they choose? Ask them to write down the name of
the animal they want to represent them today when they're happy. Then
ask them to think of the animal that represents them when they're sad.
Ask them to write down the name of that animal. Tell them that many
different things can represent how they feel and that today you're going to
ask them to think about some of those things. First, though, have them
write down the names of their happy and sad animals on the chart that
you give them. (See the sample chart in Figure 1-1.) Beside each animal
name, have them put one word that describes the animal and explains
why they chose that animal.

Student instructions for filling out the chart

Think about all the plants that you know. Plants can be flowers.
Plants can be bushes. Plants can even be trees. When you're happy,
what kind of plant are you most like? / Picture that plant in your
mind. / How big is it? / What color is it? / Where does it grow? / Do
you know its name? / Even if you do know its name, pretend that
you have just discovered this plant and have to give it a name. What
name would you give to it? / Now think of a plant that represents
what you're like when you're sad. / What does this plant look like? /
Where does it grow? / What is its name? / If you were going to name
this plant, what would be its name? / Write down the names of your
happy plant and your sad plant on your chart. Beside each one, put
one word that describes the plant and explains why you chose that
plant to represent you.

Now think about color. Look at what you're wearing today. / Are
you wearing the color that represents how you feel today? / What
color looks like you when you're happy? / What color looks like you
when you're sad? / Write down the names of those colors on your
chart. Write the words that explain why you chose those colors.

Now think about shapes. What shapes do you know? / Are you
like a circle? A triangle? A square? Are you more like a dot or a
line? Think about the shape that represents you when you're happy.
What is this shape? / Now think about the shape that represents you
when you're sad. What is this shape? Write down these shapes on
your chart. Write the words that describe these shapes on your
chart.

Now think about numbers. Count slowly, 1, 2, 3, 4, 5, 6, 7, 8, 9,
10. Which number is most like you when you're happy? / Why? /

Which number is most like you when you're sad? / Now write down the numbers that represent you on your chart. Write the words that describe why you chose these numbers.

CHART FOR THE HAPPY-SAD MANDALA

	Happy—Descriptive Word		Sad—Descriptive Word	
Animal	tiger	sunny	eagle	lonely
Plant				
Color				
Shape				
Number				

Give students large sheets of plain white paper and marking pens or crayons. (Crayon mandalas that have been laminated make vivid, beautiful creations.) Either use predrawn circles or ask students to make a large circle on their paper.

Student instructions for drawing the mandala

Today you're going to draw a picture of yourself using all of the things that you have chosen to represent you when you're happy and when you're sad. Inside your circle, you will draw pictures of your happy animal, plant, color, shape, and number. You will also draw pictures of your sad animal, plant, color, shape, and number. If your number is three, you might want to have three of your happy shapes, or three of your animals. You can use your happy color and your sad color to color your shapes or your animals. You might want to have your happy side and your sad side separate on your circle. Or you might want to mix them up, showing how your happy animal is making your sad animal feel better. Do it any way you want to, just so that all of your happy and sad *symbols* are in the circle.

When they have finished, give them the name *mandala*. Tell them that they have just made a *Happy-Sad Mandala* and that the mandala contains *symbols* that represent how they feel at two different times. After they have finished the mandalas, have them write happy-sad poems. These can be contrasting poems, such as

When I am happy,
I am a tiger,
Purring in the sunny forest,
But when I am sad,
I am an eagle,
Circling alone
In the pale blue sky.

Or they can be listing poems, such as

I am a kitten,
Playful and silly,
I am a dandelion,
Bright yellow,
A circle of one,
Happy.

I am a mouse,
Hiding in my hole,
I am a tiny blade of grass
That you can't see,
I am a black dot,
A zero,
Sad.

Be sure to display the mandalas on the wall. After students have drawn one or more mandalas for themselves and are comfortable with the concept of *symbol*, you can use the mandala to represent a character from literature. Directions are just the same except that students assume the role of the character. (See Chapter 6 for an extended treatment of literary mandalas.)

MANDALA SYMBOLIZING EMOTIONS

You might want to assign mandalas depicting emotions such as fear, anger, jealousy, or friendship. Use whatever two emotions seem appropriate to a character from a story or novel you are reading, and have students work through the mandala process. Have them talk about and write explanations of why they chose their symbols. Literary mandalas greatly enhance students' abilities to understand the motivations and interactions of characters. (See Chapter 7 for extended work with literary mandalas.) Nearly all students experience success in writing interpretive papers when the mandala work precedes the analytical.

THE GROUP MANDALA

The group mandala is another way to use this process. Students work in groups of three or four. Use large paper such as butcher paper and have them create character mandalas together. The discussion of character as they work together reflects a truly collaborative learning environment.

The metacognitive aspect of making mandalas

The making of mandalas, reinforcing as it does the foundations of reading and writing, trains students of all ages to think both visually and symbolically. It teaches and reinforces the concepts of symbol or metaphor, abstraction, and opposition. It leads from visualization and fantasy to drawing to writing, a natural progression. As students move from making metaphors (using the functions of *imagine* and *feel*) to drawing them, integrating language as appropriate (using the functions of *observe, analyze*), they're integrating various aspects of an abstraction into the graphic mandala form.

Students learn the concepts of *simile/metaphor, abstract/concrete,* and *general/specific* as they generate their images. The word search involved in the making of the mandala chart encourages precision of word choice and understanding of synonyms, antonyms, and connotations, all in the context of the student's process of uncovering the shadow images. As students construct their mandala sentences, they play with language, learning to generate sophisticated, grammatically correct sentences while integrating the various elements of their mandalas.

The act of *drawing* the mandala requires the student to show the relationships among the symbols by size, color, placement, and interaction. As students visually integrate these seemingly disparate elements of character, the developing "whole" of their mandala, like Buckminster Fuller's geodesic dome, becomes greater than the sum of its parts. They are able to see connections, to recognize the multiple layers, dimensions, and interrelationships of character, concept, and technique. This new understanding, whether conscious or subliminal, sets up a pattern of thinking that is reflected in the depth and richness of their writing.

In addition to acting as a catalyst for developing visual and metaphorical thinking behaviors, the process of comparing a character or an idea to archetypal symbols (an animal, a plant, an element), drawing the symbols, then posing reasons for their choices leads students to a deeper understanding of personality. As they begin to uncover both sun and shadow traits and to validate these traits by returning to the text, students become aware of nuances in both character and technique. They begin to see the power in what an author chooses *not* to say, and to understand how the *unsaid* as well as the *said* can be used to generate meaning. In becoming aware of these subtle personality traits, students gain insights into both cultural and personal values. This process often leads them quite naturally to compare themselves with the literary or historical characters they're studying, and, as they make these connections, they gain insight into the qualities that connect us all as members of the human community.

Sun-Symbol   Shadow-Symbol

	MOST LIKE	ADJECTIVE DESCRIBING COLUMN I	OPPOSITE OF WORD IN COLUMN II	MOST LIKE COLUMN III
ANIMAL				
PLANT				
COLOR				
NUMBER				
SHAPE				
GEM & MINERAL				
AIR EARTH ELEMENT FIRE WATER				

1-1 Sun-Shadow Mandala Chart (blank)

	Sun-Symbol			Shadow-Symbol
	MOST LIKE	ADJECTIVE DESCRIBING COLUMN I	OPPOSITE OF WORD IN COLUMN II	MOST LIKE COLUMN III
ANIMAL	Dolphin	Intelligent	Witless	Amoeba
PLANT	Sequoia	Imperious	Insignificant	Ivy
COLOR	Navy blue	Mixed	Pure	White
NUMBER	416	Complete	Unwhole	1
SHAPE	Hexagon	Multi-sided	Uniform	Circle
GEM & MINERAL	Pearl	Social	Independent	Diamond
AIR EARTH ELEMENT FIRE WATER	Water	Controlled	Wild	Fire

1-2 Sun-Shadow Mandala Chart (completed)

1-3 Personal Mandala by Tim Wong

1-4 Personal Mandala by Storm Stenvold

1-5 Personal Mandala by Judy Boshoven

CHAPTER 2

THE GRAPHIC MAP: DEFINITION AND PROCESS

A seeing and unseeing in the eye

WALLACE STEVENS

The connection between visual perception and mental processing, although not yet completely understood, is incontrovertible. Reports not only of individuals but of entire groups of people being unable to *see* that which they had not yet *conceived* abound in the literature of the past decade about the brain and perception. Lawrence Blair was one of the earliest of the current generation of researchers to tell us such stories as that of the primitive peoples who could not see Magellan's explorers arriving by boat because they had not yet conceived of the possibility of travel on the water. In the classroom we have been explorers ourselves, as we have experimented with ways to enhance our ability to *conceive* by developing our powers to *perceive*. Primary in our work has been the development of strategies to design specific visually oriented activities to generate sound thinking. The graphic map, in all of its varieties, is one of these ways.

The graphic map defined

The graphic map is a two- or three-dimensional visual construct that enables students of any age to use color, symbols, and/or words to make a unified visual interpretation or statement. It is an organizational tool through which students can make sense of a text by tracking and integrating their own ideas with words and symbols from the work they are studying.

Graphic maps range from the totally verbal map to the completely conceptual; most graphic maps, however, incorporate both symbols and words. A balanced curriculum offers many ways to express graphic thinking and incorporates them in a variety of organizational classroom configurations—individual students, groups, even whole classes.

HOW A MAP DIFFERS FROM A CLUSTER

Although at first glance, a verbal map might look like the more familiar cluster, it is created quite differently. Clustering is a process of graphic brainstorming through which students generate and collect their ideas. (See Figure 2–1.) Clustering allows students to discover what their responses and thoughts are. It helps them generate a wealth of information naturally without consciously analyzing or organizing it. The ideas represented on the cluster will, of course, connect in many ways as our thoughts flow in patterns of images. Clustering, in fact, allows students to capture the fluency of their thinking without worrying, at that time, about forming or organizing those responses. The connections, seemingly random, emerge as students begin to work with ideas generated by the clustering process.

In mapping, students discover and develop an organizational pattern for ideas and information they may have generated through clustering. Unlike the cluster, in which generating ideas is the aim, the graphic mapping process asks students to organize their thinking graphically and to validate it with symbols and/or words, drawing on direct evidence—experiential or textual—for support. We deal in this book primarily with mapping, although we use and acknowledge the immense but different value of the clustering process.

Possibilities for designing graphic map assignments reach into every discipline. In social studies, for example, students can show causal relationships, speculate, and integrate elements of a particular culture or historical period—all graphically. In science, graphic maps are familiar hallmarks, showing complex laboratory procedures or delineating such phenomena as life cycles. Venn diagrams (two interlocking circles showing the degree of overlapping information), pictures, comic strips, and graphs are common tools of mathematics students. The goal in each case is to engage students in all four functions—observe, analyze, imagine, feel—as they learn, using visual thinking to make connections to the verbal. One mark of an educated mind is the ability to translate one medium into another, to be confident in new situations, whether faced with a math problem, a poem, a student activities committee meeting, or a tennis match.

Like the mandala, the graphic map process is a catalyst for eliciting metaphorical thinking which is then, in turn, reflected in both the speaking and the writing that emerge from this process. The graphic map, however, relies more heavily on precise links to text, verbal or visual, than does the mandala. The literary graphic is different from illustrations depicting characters or setting. Students begin the graphic process with the challenge of how to organize their ideas using words and symbols drawn directly from their understanding of the text so that the finished work becomes a map of ideas rather than an illustration (see Figure 2–2).

THE VERBAL STUDY MAP

Before we introduce students to graphics using both words and symbols, we often have them make a clearly defined verbal study map. Our first directive for an assignment of a character study of Brutus in *Julius Caesar*, for example, might be "Put everything you think is important about Brutus on one side of one piece of paper." This statement immediately leads to the question, "What is important?" Students work in groups to determine categories of important facts or opinions about the character. As a class, we might decide to use three categories: personal habits and characteristics; behavior and actions; and interactions with other characters. Then, working individually or in pairs, students read through the text, finding quotations they can either quote or summarize on their map. They organize their material, decide how to place the categories, and create a map—a graphic organization of their notes. (See

Figure 2–3 for an example.) All quoted material is accompanied by its textual reference, a valuable tool for using these quotations later in papers. The verbal map is extremely useful as a notetaking or recall strategy as well as a technique for fostering interaction with a literary text.

THE VERBAL MAP INCORPORATING BASIC SYMBOLS

It is an easy step to move to a map that is primarily verbal but incorporates a clearly defined symbol from the text, often contained in the title (e.g., *The Centaur* by John Updike). (See Figure 2–4.) In this kind of map, students will begin to explore the symbol as a way of organizing their ideas.

THE CONCEPTUAL LITERARY GRAPHIC

The previous kinds of maps may be intricate and detailed or sparse and simple, but they rely on words and symbols taken directly from the text. In the conceptual literary graphic, the student integrates colors, symbols, shapes, and words that make a visual statement about a literary work or idea (see Figure 2–5). Although some conceptual graphics may be completely wordless, others may incorporate words, not as material for study, as in the verbal map, but as part of the visual statement. By presenting their graphics to the class as they lead a discussion of the work, students learn to explain choices they may have made without understanding why they made them. A graphic done completely in black and white, for instance, might be used to convey positive and negative space or emotion. While some students will make such choices consciously, often students will discover the reasons for such choices only as they explain their maps to the class. They themselves come to new understandings as they learn that all choices can be explained.

The graphic mapping process

Although the process for using graphic maps in the classroom is appropriate for many different disciplines, our examples here are drawn from literature. The literary graphic presents some aspect of a work of poetry, fiction, or drama. Students may explore such elements as character, structure, theme, or style within the framework of a single work; or they might examine the treatment of a single idea found in several works, perhaps of different genres, from different time periods or by different authors.

DEFINING PURPOSE: FINDING A FOCUS

A literary graphic assignment may be quite specific, or it might be general, urging the students to find their own direction in a text. For a general assignment such as, "Design a literary graphic for Chapter 2 of *The Red Badge of Courage*," we suggest that students begin by reviewing their initial responses to the text. They might reread their response logs (see Chapter 4 for a complete discussion of setting up reading response logs) or cluster their ideas about the chapter. Clustering and doodling are useful pre-mapping activities: through what might seem to be aimless doodling and sketching—words, pictures, symbols—students come to the knowledge of how they want to focus their graphics. It is useful to delay defining purpose and selecting a focus; frequently thought of as first steps, these difficult decisions often emerge during the process of working with the graphics. Through this unfolding process, students gain confidence in their authority as makers of meaning.

SELECTING A UNIFYING SYMBOL

Once students have settled on their topic, they select a unifying symbol or set of related symbols arising directly from the text, or from their response to it. We encourage them to trust their instincts, remembering that shapes, colors, objects, and words can all be used symbolically. Students may need reassurance at this point to let the symbol change, develop, and grow as they proceed through the graphic process. The symbol might arise directly from the text itself, such as a pig's head for a graphic of *Lord of the Flies*, or it might evolve from the kind of metaphor-making we use in the mandala process, such as a bat to represent the blind but prophetic Teiresias in *Oedipus the King*.

ASIDE: "BUT I CAN'T DRAW!"

It is at this point that we sometimes get the plaintive "But I can't draw" from students new to the graphic process. In response, we remind them that the key to a successful graphic lies in their growing understanding of the literature, not in the artistic quality of their graphic. They need to be reassured that their artistic ability will not determine the value of the process for them or for us. The primary purpose of this process is to help them think, to organize and integrate their thoughts, using parts of their brains that have, in too many cases, been dormant for many years. Many students do, of course, produce artwork of exceptional quality, and most students, given the opportunity to draw and the stimulation of other students' work, discover in themselves a powerful mode of expression. Sometimes we spend class time looking at artwork and clustering the connotations of different shapes, colors, or spacial arrangements. It's important that students begin to broaden their concept of symbol, and gain confidence in their own symbol-making ability.

REREADING FOR VALIDATING QUOTATIONS

As students begin working with the overall shape of their graphics, they return to their reading logs and to the text for quotations and examples that will validate their ideas. It isn't the number of quotations that makes a graphic effective; it's the precision with which they're chosen. Students move between text and graphic, relating to characters, events, and ideas, often in very idiosyncratic ways. It's usually with a high level of involvement that they comb the text in this process.

As students work, talking and sharing their findings, they discover various ways quotations can be incorporated into their graphics. For those literary graphics intended to be used as maps for writing papers, it's important to include textual references directly on the maps. Quotations can also be used artistically to support the visual pattern of the literary graphic. Even in totally conceptual graphics, which contain no words, students go through the same process of transacting with the text; they return regularly to the literature as they construct their graphics and refer directly to specific sections of the text as they make their presentations.

FINAL INSTRUCTIONS: INTEGRATING COLORS, SYMBOLS, WORDS

Final instructions advise students to integrate colors, symbols, and words to form a design that is pleasing and logical to them. We spend some time talking about the value of titling their work. We ask that they title, not simply label, their graphic, selecting one that will pique interest as well as suggest what the map is about.

Finding language through drawing

One of the strongest claims we make about the literary graphic process is that it deepens students' ability to think, talk, and write about literature. Both the oral presentation of graphic maps and subsequent papers demonstrate how the power of visual thinking may lead to articulate expression.

ORAL PRESENTATIONS OF GRAPHIC MAPS

Integral to the process of the graphic map is an oral presentation in which students explain their visual construct and their process of creating it. The oral process is one of growth and synthesis: as students create and execute their graphics, they discover and combine parts—symbols, shapes, colors, words—to make a cohesive whole. As they explain their arrangement or "naming of parts" to the class, they're verbally putting the parts into a larger perspective, both for themselves and for the class. During the oral presentation, students often discover that they know more than they thought they knew; the graphic process allows them to work at different levels, often coming to their final understanding only as they talk or write. Many students find that when they finally sit down to write a paper, the actual composing process has already occurred internally; in the words of one student, "the words just flowed out with a rhythm all of their own."

AN ESL STUDENT FINDS LANGUAGE THROUGH DRAWING

This first example of a student who found his way toward articulating his understanding through drawing is a senior who, as a recent immigrant, is still struggling with language problems. Through the graphic process,

Duyun learns what he has to say about Hamlet; and through both his presentation and the resulting interpretive paper, it becomes clear to him and to the class that when one has an investment in what he has to say, he will find the means to say it. Like so many ESL students in the transitional stages of learning English, Duyun is more fluent orally than he is in writing. Writing, however, sometimes takes its cue from speech; once Duyun's ideas are formulated through his oral presentation, his writing comes much more easily. To accompany the illustration of his graphic map of Hamlet (Figure 2–6, p. 52) is a portion of the transcript of Duyun's oral presentation of his graphic.

I chose to do a graphic portrayal of my understanding of the character of Hamlet. I tried to get the central idea and symbol for Hamlet for a couple of days. Finally I chose the two phases that all human beings have: the good and bad side that everyone encounters in most of their time on earth. Human beings have the tendency of imagining things and judging things in two different ways—the one favorable way and the other unfavorable way. To show this characteristic of Hamlet I tried to sketch the face of Hamlet, and then I divided his face in half to show the two sides. Then I chose my quotes and put those that seemed to be hopeful on one side and those that were not hopeful on the other side. As I looked back through the play I discovered that, not only was Hamlet depressed more than he was happy, he was most often unsure of himself—unable to make up his mind at all. These quotes I put in the middle of my graphic to show how Hamlet did a lot of wishing, but not very much acting to make his wishes happen. For instance, at one point Hamlet wanted just to kill himself so that all the pain would just end, but at the same time he wanted to face the perils that were in his path. He just often doubted the ability he possessed. To understand my graphic one must realize that the color and texture contributes, too. I chose to do my graphic with just two colors—black and white—to describe the fact that this is how Hamlet thinks. He could only see things as good or bad, but was not able to make compromises or to listen to others' advice. I think probably that Hamlet dreams in black and white, and, since we all know that dreams are one aspect of our knowing, it is logical that he would know things only in extremes. This, I think, is a major reason for his tragedy.

RELUCTANT WRITERS FIND VOICE THROUGH GRAPHICS

The graphic process marked a real turning point for two juniors in a remedial writing workshop course. These two students had spent most of the quarter scrupulously avoiding writing and even avoiding participating in class discussions. For the most part, they sat, sometimes doodling, waiting for the bell to ring. For this particular study, the class read aloud the screenplay of *Ordinary People*; they read excerpts from the novel and watched the movie. Then students began to develop graphic maps as a basis for written character studies. Paul and Ed chose to work together on this project. As they began to talk about the movie, they were shocked by the ease with which their ideas about the relationship between Conrad Jarrett and Beth, his mother, came together in their drawing. As their symbol for Beth, they chose a perfect rose with its wounding thorns, a metaphor which allowed them to account for her behavior in the story. They worked on their written character studies side by side, sharing as they wrote, and handed in their first substantive papers of the term.

Katy, a student in a junior writing workshop class, resisted the graphics assignment at first. She felt that she couldn't draw any better than she could write, yet her character map of Beth in *Ordinary People* (Figure 2–7) shows her understanding of this complex character. Like Duyun, Katy discovers her impressions of Beth as she constructs her map, uncovering the causes for Beth's mask of coldness and perfection. What is perhaps more important is that, as she makes her oral presentation, Katy discovers that she does indeed have something valid to say. The process, for her, is truly a generative one, allowing her to find and share her own voice.

In each of these instances, the students not only learned about the texts, they learned how they learn—that if they can visualize by drawing it, they can understand it. For the remainder of the semester, Duyun, Paul, Ed, and Katy sketched a great deal before they wrote. They then let their writing become an explanation for the drawing. This lesson, much more than the lesson in character analysis, was vital to their confidence and success during the rest of the year.

From the graphic map to writing

Although the graphic map may well stand on its own as an end product for a specific study, it usually leads to one or more writing assignments. Writing assignments are done individually, even when the graphic has been a group project. The group that worked together on the graphic, however, serves as an expert writing response group for its members. The writing that graphic maps generate is as wide-ranging and varied as the maps themselves. The graphic process involves the kind of thinking that leads to a variety of writing experiences: interpretation, evaluation, or analysis; style imitations, reflective essays, and poetry.

The movement from drawing to writing—imitating as it does the learning process of acquiring language—addresses the fear that often holds students back from writing or speaking in class: the deep-seated fear of not having anything to say, of sounding foolish, particularly in front of others. The self-assurance that grows with collaboration in producing a visual portrayal of ideas gives students something to say and the authority to say it. As confidence develops, grammar and correctness issues fall into perspective, resulting in papers that speak with the authenticity and ownership which you hear in Duyun's words and which you will read in other student examples throughout the book. Here are the words of one student who explains how, after completely giving up on his study of John Knowles' style, he came back to it through a metaphor that connected Knowles' style to a childhood memory:

I didn't want to do the style study paper because after failing to complete Part One (after my first semi-courageous try), I quit, resolving not to begin again. I did begin again, so that I might pass Advanced Comp. and in turn graduate. John Knowles was the author I studied. I fell in love with his unique style, but for the life of me I couldn't figure out what it was. I wrote my parallel story without knowing. I did write with some of his more obvious traits but his real style, the style which comes from the inner sentence, eluded me.

That style was not apparent to me until I completed the graphic analysis. At least it was not too late to include in my oral report. At any rate, his style consists of long complex sentences which hold many different, non-related ideas separated within the sentence by commas, and the whole sentence is held together often only by one small phrase. As I took one of his sentences apart and put each of the parts on my blank paper, separately, I thought of when I was a kid and I liked to sit and watch the trains go by our back yard. Suddenly the sentence seemed to me to be like the train. Each part was separate, had a different function. Some cars carried coal, others people. The wheels were like the commas, and the whole thing had a sound, a rhythm that I just loved. I took some of Knowles' sentences and drew them as separate cars of a train, stretching out across my page. An example of a sentence like that is:

> *"An evening wind was mussing the crowded*
> *leaves on the trees, study-lamp light shone*
> *from the rooms in Jonathan Edwards College*
> *as he strolled past it, feeling strange,*
> *outcast, fugitive." from Paragon, p. 29*

The sentence is perfect. It is a collection of four separate "cars" held together by the information "as he strolled past it." Furthermore, each thought adds its own element to the mood of the sentence which is set by the words "feeling strange, outcast, fugitive," the same mood I used to feel as I watched the trains.

EXTRACT FROM DEAN ALEXANDER'S PAPER

The metacognitive aspect of map-making

Constructing a graphic map engages students in all of the four functions. As students construct a graphic map, they're responding to the impact of color and design as well as to the content of the text, using the *feeling* function. They engage in close *observation* as they peruse the text for validating quotations. They stretch for their symbols, using the *imagine* function, synthesizing their impressions and ideas as they *analyze* and organize their ideas. Each student has the opportunity to work comfortably in the mode most natural to her or him and at the same time to experience and develop the other modes.

One of the most exciting benefits of the literary graphic activity is that it provides for, in Louise Rosenblatt's words, "the gradual discovery of ideas and insights by the student through actual literary experience and reflection upon it." This discovery is, of course, true, regardless of whether the subject matter of the map is a literary work or a scientific concept and regardless of whether the student is in fifth grade or college. Throughout the entire mapping process students are actively transacting with the text through integrated reading, writing, speaking, and listening activities. Students might begin by trying to shape their graphic—by trying to produce a product; however, in a short time, quite naturally, the process takes over and students release control, letting go of their preconceptions and allowing the map to shape itself. They find themselves molding and changing symbols, colors, ideas, and concepts and re-observing both themselves and their subject at every step. They're discovering the aesthetic, cultural, and ethical values in the work *themselves*, rather than depending on the teacher or secondary sources to give them "right" answers.

The mapping process makes in-depth reading a natural process as students formulate their ideas, construct their maps, and return to the text for validation. As students create the overall shape and symbolic pattern of their graphic, they begin to think metaphorically, to see the abstract as well as the literal, and to develop a visceral understanding of the whole and of the parts that make up that whole.

In *Don Quixote*, Cervantes said that you can "journey over all the universe in a map, without the expense and fatigue of traveling, without suffering the inconveniences of heat, cold, hunger and thirst." I'm not certain that students of the graphic map would completely agree that it's "without fatigue" and "without suffering"; however, they will acknowledge that creating a graphic map carries them on a multi-pathed "journey over all the universe."

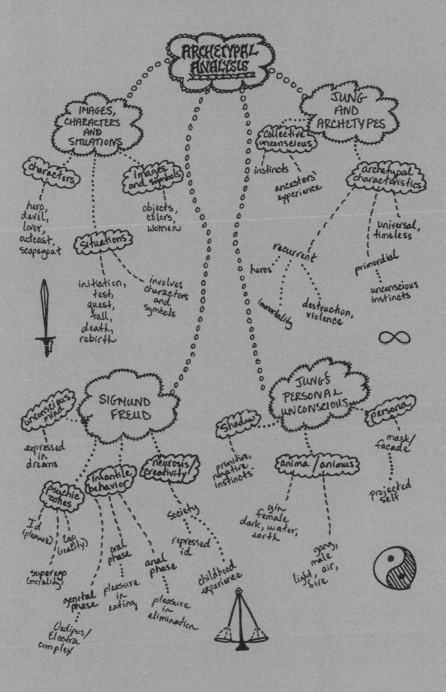

2-1 Cluster for Test: Archetypal Analysis by Bonnie Morey

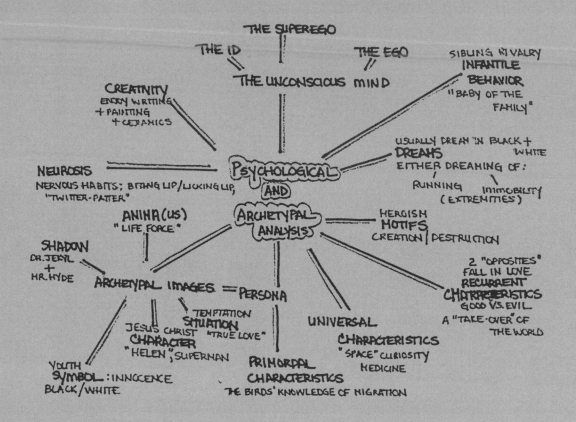

2-2 Map: Psychological and Archetypal Analysis
by Ann Ratto

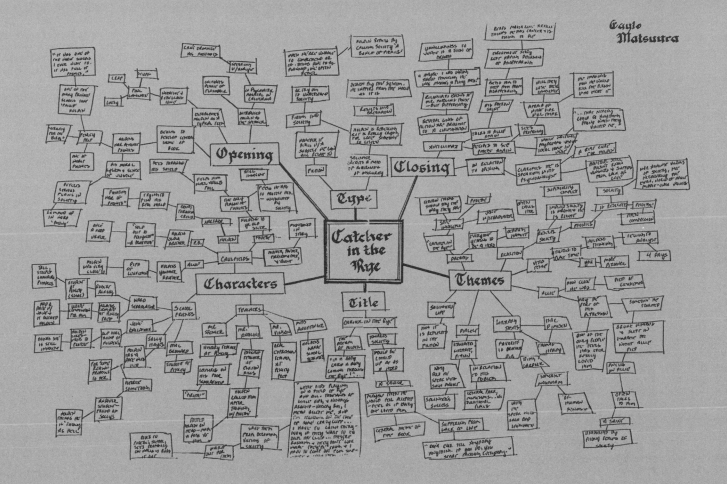

2-3 The Verbal Strategy Map: *Catcher in the Rye*
by Gayle Matsuura

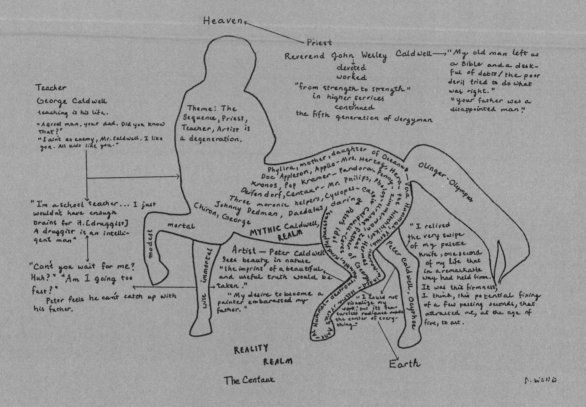

2-4 The Verbal Map with Symbol: *The Centaur* by Betty Wong

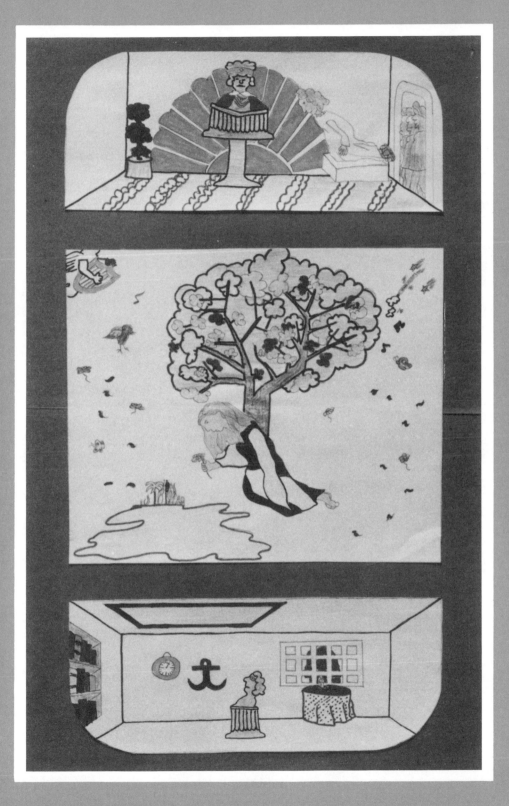

2-5 Conceptual Graphic for *The Apple Tree* by Linda Yee

2-6 An ESL Student Finds Language Through Drawing:
Hamlet by Duyun Hwang

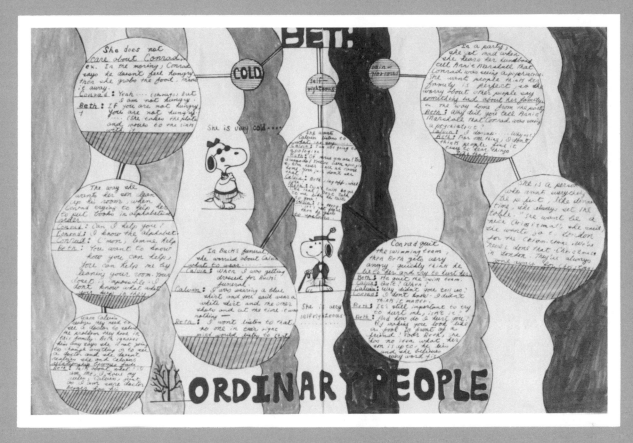

2-7 Reluctant Writer Finds Voice Through Graphics:
Beth from *Ordinary People* by Katy Lee

A

B

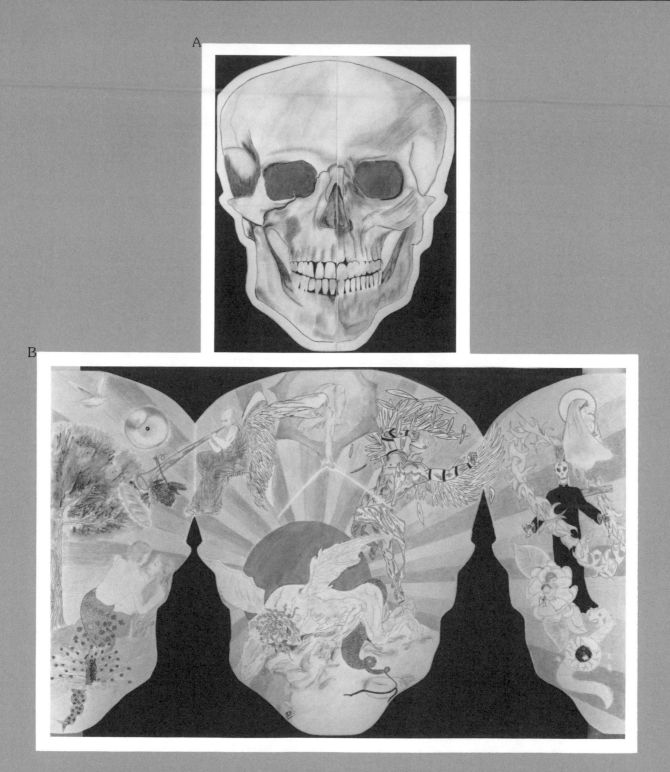

Portrait of the Artist by Anita Wong, Thorsten Anderson, and John Williams

PART TWO

PROCESS AND PRODUCT: WHEN, WHY, AND HOW

The edgings and inchings of final form

WALLACE STEVENS

Process and product

The bright new edge of the word *process* has become almost lost in the new wave of educational reform like so many ideas that become inextricably tied to a word or phrase. *The writing process*, for example, has become shorthand for the many different acts and activities that we do when we write. The danger is that what begins in an attempt to describe may end up as a directive to prescribe. On the other hand, in the scramble to champion "the process approach," many teachers have become shy of talking about *product*, as if attending to a finished work were somehow slightly suspect. In Part II, we emphasize the processes of using graphics—both mandalas and maps—in various stages of working through a book or a unit, but we don't stop with process. We assume that a product, or products, will result from all of our classroom activity and that we will be able to assess these products, to assess the process that went into their making, and, perhaps most important of all, to help students understand and evaluate their own processes and products.

Classroom management

Essentially, Part II will deal with the specifics of classroom management: why to use one kind of graphic here, another there; why to have some graphics done by groups and others by individuals; when to stop the reading of a novel for a quick graphic and when not to; when to use what graphic form; and how to structure the classroom to integrate graphics into the curriculum.

Students with special needs

As we move through the processes of getting started and integrating graphics into the study of literature, we will specify how graphics can have particular significance for students with special needs (*all* students, in our book). The student who is learning English as a second language, the learning disabled, the language-reluctant, the Advanced Placement student, the turned-off student, the euphemistically *general* student—all have special needs that can be at least addressed directly in some way through the processes that we detail in Part II.

Visual learning has important implications for all students. It already has a strong educational base for the learning disabled student as a precursor to reading and writing. Less well-known, however, is its potential to provide

55

a much-needed balance for the overly linear "successful" student. These students are often fearful of coloring outside the lines, of moving beyond the crutch of the formulaic essay. When they begin to take risks, to venture however tenuously outside the lines, they are on their way toward becoming intellectually independent. Those students who feel that school has no claim on their lives may find the physical act of drawing a steadying, calming activity that gives them a sense of achievement, of believing in their own power to make meaning of unfamiliar texts (of English, of school). We have found that our very high percentage of ESL students is able to demonstrate the complexities of their interpretive abilities directly through graphic assignments and that working with other students to make presentations to the class helps them make transitions to English. We certainly don't mean to imply that using graphics is a panacea to the overwhelmingly profound problems facing the many constituencies of our schools today; but we do believe that integrating these strategies into one's repertoire of available ways of teaching to the variety of student needs that face us can make a significant difference.

Incorporating visual thinking and the graphic process into the classroom helps create a climate in which there can be no failure; a climate in which all students come to take responsibility for their own learning. It provides a starting point for class discussion; it teaches students to read closely; it encourages students to look back at text, to re-view it from different perspectives; and through group presentations, it allows students to teach each other.

The role of the teacher

In such a climate, the role of the teacher is critical, requiring not only our firm stance in the power of our subject matter but also a trust in the processes of talking, writing, and drawing as essential elements of the way we learn. As students work on group graphics, we find ourselves moving easily from group to group, asking a question of one, sharing a personal interpretation with another, perhaps sitting down to tackle a difficult section with a third. During student presentations, we participate in the class discussion, adding observations or raising questions. At the same time, we are, of course, continually assessing not only the presenters, but the rest of the class, looking for the evidence of learning—probing minds, involvement, insights, articulateness, metaphorical and critical thinking.

The question of assessment

The question of assessment inevitably comes up in teacher workshops on using graphics, and rightly so. Our evaluations are heavily dependent on observations of student involvement and evidence of creative and analytical thinking during the individual or group work of discussion, writing, and presentation. The graphic products are assessed as part of the presentation, whether it is oral or written or both. We don't grade the artistic quality of the graphic, although one of us admits to having a "fame and glory wall" where graphics of dazzling beauty (determined by the class by acclamation) remain in long-term exhibition to let us enjoy those special talents among us. The fame-and-glory graphics receive the maximum number of points, but so do many others that are considerably less artistic.

The process log

We find it extremely helpful to have students keep a process log in which they record their day-to-day work in the class. They simply log what they have done, both in class and at home, and note progress or questions about their current projects. These logs are distinct from their reading logs or other kinds of journals that we might assign, take moments to check, and keep us up to date on any problems that students might be experiencing either individually or with the functioning of their groups.

Self-assessment

We believe strongly in helping students learn the art of self-assessment. To that end, our students keep folders of all their work during the term; at the end of the term, they take the responsibility for designing a portfolio of work that they value, along with a written (often with a graphic component) evaluation of their participation and their learning. In many classes we assign an end of the term graphic, the culmination of an individual or group study that has been maintained as an ongoing study project throughout the semester or year.

We propose, then, to honor both process and product, recognizing the dangers of suggesting that one should begin with *this* and end with *that*. As Ezra Pound says in *ABC of Reading*, if your goal is to make a three-legged stool, it doesn't much matter which leg you start with. Still, there are some progressions that seem useful as we try to make sense of the developmental aspect of metaphoric thinking. In Part II, we share our understanding of how, when, and why we use graphics in the classroom and how the management of this process actually decreases the paper load while augmenting the curriculum.

CHAPTER 3

GETTING STARTED: MAKING AN ABSTRACTION CONCRETE

Not ideas about the thing, but the thing itself

WALLACE STEVENS

There are, of course, many ways to build a three-legged stool of visual and metaphoric thinking. Ideally, our entire curriculum, pre-school through graduate school, would be structured in such a way that students would grow up calling easily on whatever thinking behavior was appropriate to the situation. Students would be able to visualize their reading, incorporate imagery and metaphorical thinking into their writing, be as much at home with a poem or an essay as with a video game or a movie. Ironically, kids growing up today are at home with many aspects of the visual world, but often in a completely passive way. They don't generate the images they see on the screen. They don't think up the clever video games. They don't engage in actively making sense of how they fit into that world of vivid color and moving shapes.

We don't pretend that using graphics in the classroom will magically make it possible for students to see the connections between movies and the mind, between life and books, but we believe that it will at least help activate their powers of thinking visually and metaphorically—a step toward translating the visual world they are surrounded by into a world they have helped create.

Making an abstraction concrete

This one-period activity provides an easy introduction to the concepts *abstract* and *concrete*. We introduce it at some point when we are talking about specific values, emotions, or themes important to a specific work of literature. It would be equally applicable to a study of concept in science, history, or math.

THE PROCESS

Working first with the class to demonstrate the process, we ask that students select abstractions from the list or cluster that they have generated as a small group or class in discussing the themes in a novel. They suggest *power, frustration, selflessness*. We then ask them to *draw* their abstract word. What concrete images could exemplify their abstraction? What is *power* like? They begin to doodle images. One student draws a sword. Another a broken umbrella. Why a sword? "Power is like a two-edged sword," the student responds. We move then from the direct simile to the straightforward, more forceful metaphor: "Power *is* a two-edged sword," one student quickly replies. "Frustration *is* a broken umbrella in a hard rain," someone adds, moving from her drawing directly to the metaphor.

With plain white paper and lots of colored markers available, students choose one abstraction from their own list and begin drawing. As you can see in the examples (Figures 3–1 and 3–2), they go beyond mere illustration and actually express metaphorical concepts. Noelle's rainbow is not just the ubiquitous adolescent rainbow; her drawing conveys the ephemeral quality of life by showing the rainbow both in vivid and in pale, disappearing hues. Peace is depicted as "a balloon in the wind," a concept that becomes meaningful when we see that the map on Derek's drawing is a sketch of Israel and Lebanon.

When they have finished their drawings (fifteen or twenty minutes is enough for this activity), they write an extended metaphor, which often takes the shape of a short poem. In this sequence of activity the subtleties of the metaphor emerge: abstraction, drawing, a sentence containing an elaboration of the initial concrete image.

One memorable response to this assignment was a metaphorical representation of the abstraction "depression." The student drew a forest that had been ravaged by fire—black spines of trees towering over barren ground. Above the desolation, enclosed in a cloudlike boundary, the student drew a green, living forest. With no words, this student conveyed his understanding of depression: the burned-out forest itself is not representative of depression unless one has a memory of the forest as it had been.

A surrealistic game

The surrealists used to gather in the cafes and play art or word games that forced improbable but felicitous conjunctions of thought. The reasoning behind their lighthearted approach to art was a belief that making connections is a primary act of human intelligence. We agree in this respect with the artists. Pick any three words at random from the dictionary and we can make some connections. We begin here with a whole-class surrealistic game activity to clarify the meaning of the words *abstract* and *concrete* by integrating a drawing into the game.

THE PROCESS

First, we brainstorm or cluster abstract nouns, emphasizing that an abstract noun must be the name of something that we cannot see, touch, taste, hear, smell. If we cannot perceive it through the senses, how can we know it? This question often leads to a discussion of how we know anything that we don't perceive sentiently, and that leads to speculations: by using examples; by making connections. After a short discussion, we select one of the abstract nouns at random and circle it on the board. We'll select *anger*.

Next, we brainstorm or cluster concrete nouns, clarifying the term *concrete* by beginning with the things we can see in the classroom, then moving to other things that are very much a part of students' lives. Again, we select one concrete noun at random to demonstrate how to play the game. Let's say we select *desk*.

Using these two words, we try to think up all of the possible ways that we could define the abstract noun in terms of the concrete. How is *anger* like a *desk*? We list as many possibilities as students can think of in just two or three minutes.

Anger is like a desk

... because it is hard.
... because it has deep grooves in it.
... because a lot of different people experience it.
... because you don't want to be behind it.

When we have a number of similes, we ask each student to make up one sentence comparing anger to a desk. We ask them to take out the word *like* and make the comparison direct: "Anger *is* a desk...." We then share these sentences quickly in pairs, maybe with a few read to the whole class. We might get a sentence like "Anger is a wooden desk, hard and unyielding, scarred, with deep grooves made by all of the different people that have experienced sitting behind it over the years." Students are then ready for an elaboration of the game.

INSTRUCTIONS FOR A SURREALISTIC GAME

1. Numbering from 1 to 10, list ten abstract nouns, preferably words that express some value or emotion.
2. Cover your list. Now, numbering again, list ten concrete nouns.
3. Using the base sentence "Anger is a wooden desk ..." as a frame, find points of similarity between the abstract noun and the concrete noun *having the same number*. Create a simile for each abstraction, making the connection explicit. You are honor-bound to use the two words with the same number.
4. Select the three similes that you like best and share them with a partner. Then, working with your partner, change the similes into extended metaphors. You may find that your original comparison becomes quite different as you play with extending the ideas, making them into sentences.
5. Choose one of your metaphors and, using color, shape, and design, draw the concrete aspect of it. Integrate the abstract word and your sentence into your graphic. (See Figure 3–3.)

Notan: Visualizing positive and negative space

The Japanese concept of *notan* gives us a quick perception assignment to help students visualize positive and negative space. We pass out pieces of white and black construction paper, scissors, and tape. The purpose is to construct a design in which neither black nor white is dominant to the eye. The perfectly constructed example of notan, like the work of Escher, will present a perceptual puzzle for the viewer. Which do you look at, white or black? Which is foreground, background? Can you hold both images in your mind at the same time? These questions give rise to questions of positive and negative space in other art forms, in music, in science, and in poetry.

We have found that the notan assignment, while it takes only a class period, including discussion, is one that students frequently refer to as we move through the year. The theme of dualities, echoed in the sun-shadow mandala, recurs as one of the dominant themes in literature—the dualities of war and peace, of love and hate, of appearance and reality. Escher provides an example of the balance of positive and negative space characteristic of notan (Figure 3–4).

Mandala metaphors and modeling

This assignment in using metaphor can be used at any point in the year. We introduce it here as another way of making abstractions concrete. If students have already completed a personal sun-shadow mandala, you can draw on their understanding of images, but it isn't essential that the mandala exercise precede this one. We begin here with instructions for integrating graphics with modeling a poem; the second assignment integrates the modeling of a poem with the study of a novel or play.

MODELING A POEM (Assignment #1)

Begin by giving each student a copy of the poem and reading it aloud:

LULLABY FOR A DAUGHTER

Go to sleep.   Night is a coalpit full of black water.
        Night is a dark cloud full of warm rain.
Go to sleep.   Night is a flower resting from bees.
        Night is a green sea swollen with fish.
Go to sleep.   Night is a white moon riding her mare.
        Night is a bright sun burned to black cinder.
                        Go to sleep.
                Night's come.
                    Cat's day
                    Owl's day
            Star's feast of praise
                Moon to reign over
        Her sweet subject, dark.

                            JIM HARRISON

After reading the lullaby poem aloud, have students record words, phrases, or lines that they are struck by. Ask them to respond to their recorded words with a quickdraw (a sketch), then with their own written reactions.

Introduce the idea of their writing a poem of their own, modeled after the lullaby poem.

Instructions to students

1. Select a key word, an abstraction, or a concept that is important to you. The key word in the poem is "night," but you may choose any word that you want.
2. Select six concrete images as metaphors for your key word. You might want to use different categories from the sun-shadow mandala assignment, such as *animal, plant, minerals or gems,* or elements such as *air, earth, fire,* and *water.*
3. Write a sentence for each of the concrete images.
4. Look at the poem again and notice the phrase that serves as a refrain: "Go to sleep." Think about your key word and compose a brief refrain for your poem. Write it using the imperative, as the author of "Lullaby" does. (The *imperative* form of a verb is a directive to someone to do something: *Be still. Shut the door. Don't go away.*)
5. You have a refrain, an abstraction, and six concrete images with sentences for each. (In the poem, there are six concrete images for "night.") Now you have all you need to model this poem, following its form but using your own ideas. You may need to confer with members of your writing group when you get to the second part of the poem; it's more difficult, but you should have enough ideas to play with and come up with an interesting finish of your own.
6. For publication, make a mandala, a circle; draw all of your images inside it. On the same paper, write out your poem. Be sure to title and sign your work.

STUDENT EXAMPLES OF MODELS TO "LULLABY FOR A DAUGHTER"

This model was written to a friend who needed comfort:

TO SUSAN

Take comfort.   Warmth is an old time melody
                                playing softly over the radio.
            Warmth is a bathtub bursting with bubbles.
Take comfort.   Warmth is a well-worn teddy bear
                                left over from childhood.
            Warmth is a bucket of ripe, red apples.
Take comfort.   Warmth is a drawer
                                full of worn-out jeans.
            Warmth is a mouthful of homemade cookies
                                on a rainy day.

Take comfort.
Warmth is all around
Vulcan's might.
Night's rival.
Flame's heavenly glow.
Ash's final gift,
Fire's child, warmth.

JENNIFER OLSON

In "Assignment for a Class," Thomas Hudson plays with the assignment and assumes the voice of the teacher.

ASSIGNMENT FOR A CLASS

Model this poem.   Poetry is a tall glass of words.
      Poetry is emotion spilled out on paper.
Model this poem.   Poetry is the noise of a brook in the woods.
      Poetry is alcohol that pickles your brain.
Model this poem.   Poetry is color represented in black and
      white.   Poetry is a tree bending in the wind.
                  Model this poem.
            Humanities is here.
                  Poetry writing
                  Literary analysis
            A writer's chance to shine
                  Teacher to reign over
            Her patient subject, learning.

THOMAS N. HUDSON

The next example, "March to Drums," was written as an exercise for students to observe their own process of working through an assignment in modeling. We sometimes have students keep what we call a "metacognitive journal" as they are doing an assignment as a way of helping them understand their own mental processes. We ask students to draw a line down the center of the page as they do for other double entry journal entries. They work on the assignment itself in the left hand column; in the right, they record whatever goes through their minds as they work. Later, they reread their logs and write a short reflective paper about how they approached the assignment. We include here the reflective notes from Enrique Barot's journal after he modeled this poem.

March to drums. War is a firecracker,
      brilliantly connived.
   War is a harsh teacher with a fatal stick.

March to drums. War is a callous game.
   War is a machine spewing red smoke.

March to drums.   War is a hurricane
       which sweeps up all.
     War is a faceless enemy that will win.
       March to drums.
   War's here.
     Soldier's cry.
     Nation's cry.
   Guns scream in glee
  Hatred gives orders to
her faceless child, war.

REFLECTIVE NOTES

Never before have I really put down in a tactile way the process by which I arrive at a finished, polished piece of writing. A teacher once said I was an internal writer, meaning that what I had written down is it, mistakes are usually gone, and the meaning of the thoughts all processed and revised in the head, never on paper.

This assignment of metacognition gave me a chance to really see in writing what I thought about everything I was thinking about. All through the lullaby poem I got this incredibly soothing, secure feeling. It made darkness seem like such a friend.

For my own poem, war was a first choice. The imagery of blood and soldiers as my primary ideas I didn't like, but once I got down to metaphors, I felt I was an arm's length away from war again. Jonah and the whale compared to war was my first metaphor, but in the end, thoughts of gentle, old blue whales did not satisfy my gross ideas of war. As I dug deeper and deeper still, I thought of firecrackers and grinding machines, and gods' wrath, and rabid dogs. I saw screams and chess pieces, and bloody rushing smoke. I mean, wow!

March to drums. That seemed to be the most appropriate accompaniment to the somber metaphors of war. In thinking of marching and dreams, I saw faceless soldiers draped in black and red, marching silently to the sound of ominous drums while tempests terrorize the heavens. Heavy stuff.

"Soldiers cry, nations cry, guns scream in glee, hatred gives orders to her faceless child, war." I believe those are the best lines of the poem.

ENRIQUE BAROT

INTEGRATING THE MODEL WITH THE STUDY OF LITERATURE
(Assignment #2)

As a class, cluster ideas that play a major part in a novel or play. Look for such ideas as frustration, jealousy, ambition, apathy, idealism, love, war, childhood; or look for such abstractions as loneliness, separation, prejudice, fear, time. Talk about these ideas as abstractions, things that exist, that provide motivation for the way we behave, but that we can't understand unless they're made concrete for us by pictures or actions.

Instructions for students

1. Select one of the big themes and write as many concrete images as possible for this abstraction. Look first for symbols or images from the work you have been studying. If you select an action, treat it like a stop-action on a camera so that you can describe it in detail. Make these true images—things you can picture in your mind, things you could draw.
2. Go through your list and select six of these images. Then write six sentences, each beginning _____ (your abstraction) is _____ (an extended description of your image).
3. Put your work aside for a few minutes and listen to this poem:
   (Read or reread "Lullaby for a Daughter.")
4. Now look at the poem again and notice the phrase that serves as a refrain: "Go to sleep." Think about the main character in the work that you have been studying and compose a brief refrain for your poem addressed to this character. Write it in the imperative, as the author of "Lullaby" does.
5. You have a refrain, an abstraction, and six concrete images with sentences for each. (In the poem, there are six concrete images for "night.") Now you have all you need to model this poem, following its form but using your own ideas. You may need to confer with members of your writing group when you get to the second part of the poem; it is more difficult. But you should have enough ideas to play with and come up with an interesting finish of your own.
6. For publication, make a mandala, using the concrete images, and place it on a single page with an edited copy of your poem. Be sure to title and sign your work.

This poem is addressed to Creon, after a study of Sophocles' *Antigone*.

SEE THE MISTAKES

Open your eyes.   Creon is as stubborn as a mule.
        Creon is as hollow as a piece of bamboo.
Open your eyes.   Creon is bold like the color black.
        Creon is as complex as the number 2,817,435,091.
Open your eyes.   Creon is a sharp bitter man not listening to
                                    anyone.
        Creon is like fire, inexorable and relentless.
                        Open your eyes.
            Creon's edict.
                    Antigone's death.
                    Haemon's death.
            Eurydice's fatal suicide.
                    See the mistakes.
        Creon, open your eyes.

ROBERT DENIRO

SUGGESTIONS FOR OTHER DISCIPLINES

From the field of art:

Find six paintings, sculptures, or other art forms that deal with the same subject. Using that common subject, find an image from each of the artworks for the metaphors of the poem.

From the field of science:

From a fieldnotes observation, select an animal or plant, rather than an abstraction, as your base word. For example, "The *fox* is a strip of sun, vanishing into the trees."

From the field of history:

Select a historical time period as your base word. For example, "The West in 1849 was a rainbow with a pot of gold just over the next hill."

CONCLUSION

There is no one way or right way of getting started, of introducing graphics to a class. So much depends on the age of the students, their experiences with metaphorical thinking, your own goals, the time of year. We like to begin very early in September, to set the pattern, to make it natural for students to pick up the marking pens, to put their work on the wall. We want students to be comfortable with the physical aspects of using color and shape and understand the relationship of what they draw to what they think, say, or write.

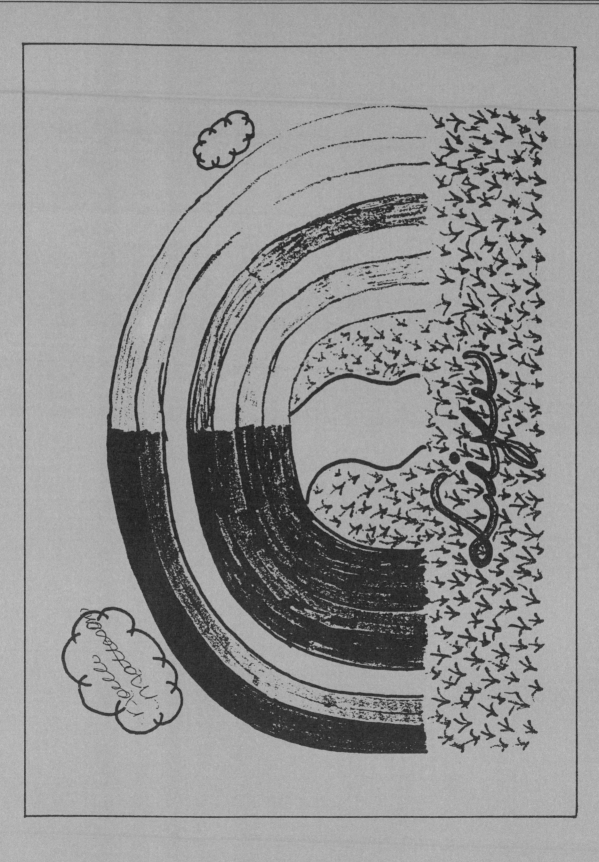

3-1 "Life" by Noelle Matteson

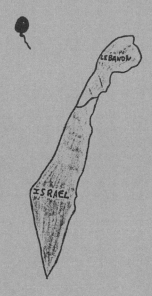

Peace Is A Ballon In The Wind

3-2 "Peace" by Derek Taner

3-3 "Frustration" by Patty La Rosa

3-4 "Positive and Negative Space" — M.C. Escher

CHAPTER 4

GRAPHICS AND THE STUDY OF LITERATURE

Jot these milky matters down. They nourish Jupiters.

WALLACE STEVENS

Before we begin working through a text, part by part, we often have students read through an entire work quickly just for the story line. Sometimes, however, we slow down even the first reading, providing frameworks that invite students to interact verbally and graphically with the text as they read. These initial jottings and sketchings become a record of students' first responses to the text and provide important connections for later, more intense, study. The quick-draws and quick-maps of the early study engender the high level of involvement that produces the graphics, presentations, and writing for a unit.

Visual note-taking and note-making

THE QUICK-DRAW

As students read through a work that they are going to study in some depth, they keep a *reading log*. Part of this log includes the *quick-draw*, a sketch that marks a critical stage in the development of metaphorical thinking. For an introductory example of a log entry with a quick-draw, see Figure 4–1.

The process of logging begins with the selection of a specific quotation or an event in the assigned reading. Here are the steps in the process:

Instructions for reading log with quick-draw:

1. Select a quotation or an event that you wish to respond to.
2. Place the quotation in context.
3. Write a personal response to the quotation.
4. Find some general significance in the ideas you are exploring.
5. Do a quick-draw that crystallizes the central idea in the quotation.
6. Explain how the quick-draw relates to the text.

The sequenced sections of this kind of reading log impel the student to move first from the text to context; then from a personal response to a more general or universal significance; and finally, from a quick-draw back to the text through a written explanation of the metaphoric implications of the sketch.

A sample reading response log: Instructions to students

1. Text Selection: Choose a brief quotation or an event from your assigned reading. Copy the quotation or briefly summarize the event on your paper. Include the chapter and page number.

STUDENT RESPONSE:

"A writhing horror twisted itself across his features, like a snake gliding swiftly over them, and making a little pause, with all its wreathed intervolutions in open sight." The Scarlet Letter, *Chapter 2*

2. Contextual Placement: Explain the meaning and/or importance of this quotation to the story. You might paraphrase it and tell what it shows about the character(s) and/or plot. It may raise questions in your mind. It may remind you of something that happened or was said earlier in the text; it may provide you wit. .ints of something to come. Your comments here should be based on how this quotation functions in the story, and, particularly, in this chapter of the story.

STUDENT RESPONSE

Having learned of Hester's transgressions, this strange man has suddenly become incredibly angry. He must know Hester well, for rarely are emotions like anger so uncontrollable. However no one witnesses this anger because it flits across his face so quickly. Still, the reader inevitably ponders his own emotions now, after reading this peculiar description, and Hawthorne uses this tickler to build the tension in the story. I really want, now, to know more about this strange and rather sinister man.

3. Personal Response: Tell what *you* think of the idea or situation you selected. Explore your own reactions to the meaning of the quotation, or to the situation or feelings of the character. Have you ever felt similar things, known a similar or parallel situation?

STUDENT RESPONSE

Sometimes when I suddenly come into an emotion-causing situation, the emotion bursts upon me like a wave, cresting and pulling me in over my head. Like the waves, the emotions take me over and overwhelm me, until, fighting the undertow, I can pull my head above the water. It seems that this is what happened to the man. He came unexpectedly upon something that caused him so much anger, he found it uncontrollable for an instant. Although he, like me, soon gained footing in the wet sand of cold reason, his malice showed through temporarily. It's often the unpreparedness of the emotion that catches me off-guard, and this unpreparedness, the not being able to "entrench" yourself, makes the loss of composure that much more complete.

4. Reflective Response: Tell what you think this quotation says about people and/or the world in general. Here, try to see how this situation is typical of what people feel or experience in their lives. Make a broad, general connection here.

Everyone does, at one time or another, come across an emotion with which they are unable to grapple. They come across, almost always accidentally, an emotional situation for which they aren't prepared. Hester, although flung violently into a high emotional situation, was able to prepare for these and embarrassment she would face, and therefore she could withdraw and not show her emotions. The man who inquires after what she has done, however, has no such preparation. His anger leaps straight to his face where it "twisted itself across his features" until he was able to control it. For him, as for everyone, emotion can come as a surprise. It must be known to be controlled.

5. Quick-Draw: Sketch, in ink or in color, a symbol for the quotation or event you've chosen. The drawing need not be elaborate, but it should show some relationship to the meaning or feelings of the quotation. Explain your drawing; tell why you chose the symbol, colors, etc. that you did. (See Figure 4–2.)

STUDENT RESPONSE

Sudden emotion is like a storm. If one's prepared for it, he might be able to retreat to a house or some type of shelter, as Hester, to avoid it. If, however, one is unprepared, like the man, the deluge will engulf him and he'll definitely become soaked.

As students work through the first stages of the log, they make connections from the text to themselves, then place their own responses in a larger context. These connections are often tentative, but students are engaged in all of the learning functions—observe, analyze, imagine, feel—as they choose a quotation or event, discover a parallel in their own lives, and draw a metaphoric connection. The act of drawing forces students to visualize, to *imagine*, this connection. After the students have sketched the metaphor, they articulate the connection embedded in the drawing.

Such activities don't take more than twenty to thirty minutes for students to do. Since we assign logging regularly as an adjunct to assigned reading, students learn to let their thoughts flow naturally and quickly, logging their reactions as they reflect and interpret. As they begin to trust their initial responses, they risk more sophisticated responses to the text. Making connections between literature and their lives gives them a real ownership of the text and deepens their understanding of the power of literature.

For the reluctant reader or the ESL student, the sketch can be a catalyst unlocking the ability to articulate thoughts. Though often unable at first to express an opinion about a book, these students *do* know what they feel. When we ask them to do a quick-draw of a moving or pivotal part of a work, we allow them to begin their study by imagining and feeling, modes that do not require facility in language. They can, in this way, capture their responses without the interference of language. It becomes much easier then for these students to explain their drawings and their relationship to the story, a first step toward helping these students realize and recognize their own responses.

STUDENT RESPONSES TO THE READING LOG/ QUICK-DRAW ASSIGNMENT

Although students can use any aspect of a night's reading as a stimulus for a reading log, it's important that they choose their own focus. Such choice gives them a commitment to the literature, an investment that intensifies as they work through the book using the log. In Figure David, a freshman, bases his log on a short quotation from Chapter 3 of Steinbeck's *The Pearl:*

For it is said that humans are never satisfied, that you give them one thing and they want something more. And this is said in disparagement, whereas it is one of the greatest talents the species has and one that has made it superior to animals that are satisfied with what they have. (p. 32)

David's log leads him to consider greed in the novel, in himself, and more generally in the world. His quick-draw, (Figure 4–3) in black and white, brings the focus back to the text, showing his integration of text, self, and world.

David's log entry:

This graphic represents the result of greed. The man is devoid of color because it represents his soul as it is corrupted away, as Kino's soul is becoming corrupted. As he puts all of his faith in the material instead of other people, he looks to the pearl to see the future. The pearl becomes his crystal ball. Wispy images float across it as he intently watches, closing out everything else. This obsession, triggered by his greed, leads to distrust, then to paranoia as his soul disappears. Yet still, he looks into the pearl, clasping it with all of his might.

Kirby, a junior, bases his log on the episode in Book 1 of Cather's *My Antonia* in which Jim, in a panicked attack, kills a snake with a spade. In his log, Kirby says, "Most people have, at one point or another, an experience that changes their outlook on life. Through killing the snake Jim can finally believe he is worthy of respect. He knows that he 'had killed a big snake . . . and was now a big fellow.' "

His quick-draw, a simple sketch of an open door through which a sunlit hill is seen, is accompanied by the following explanation:

This rite of passage opens many doors for Jim. He feels he has a better command of his life, and can take advantage of these opportunities, and this confidence aids him both in his own life and in his relationship with others, such as Antonia.

Danielle Yee, a junior, chose John Updike's poem "Ex-Basketball Player" as the focus for her log. We had not studied the poem as a class; rather, students had been asked to find a poem that reflected in some way the theme of isolation that we had been following through such works as *The*

Scarlet Letter and *Catcher in the Rye*. In her log, Danielle responds to Flick's loneliness as he focuses on his past glory as a high school basketball star. Her sketch is very simple, a full-length mirror standing alone in a room. Her explanation, however, shows clearly her understanding of the poem and her ability to draw connections between disparate works.

When you look in a mirror, you are only able to see what is behind you—not what is ahead of you. This mirror is reflective of Updike's "Ex-Basketball Player," showing how Flick, like everyone else who is stuck in a rut, gets caught and is only able to relate to the past. There are so many ways of being isolated. Hester is ostracized by society, and Holden ostracizes society, holding himself apart from it. Flick Webb, on the other hand, is isolated by his inability to change and to look forward and grow with the times.

Whether the stimulus for the log is a quotation, an event, or a general response to an entire poem or short work, the process and the results are the same: the writing, the drawing, and the subsequent explanation generate significant connections between literature and life.

THE CARDS: AN EXERCISE IN INTERPRETATION

One of the most difficult aspects of teaching interpretive thinking and writing is helping students internalize the difference between what a passage *says* and what it *does* in the text. Just as the quick-draw is effective in helping students visualize connections between themselves, a text, and the world, here, too, the quick-draw can be a valuable tool in helping students recognize what a passage does to contribute to the meaning of the whole. Students work individually or in groups to interpret and analyze substantial sections of a work. Our focus here is on helping them see beyond the plot line as they consider and show graphically how each part contributes to the meaning and effect of the whole. (See Figures 4–4 and 4–5 for examples.)

Instructions for making the interpretive cards

Choose an event or quotation from the assigned reading. Follow these steps using a 5″ × 8″ card:

1. Note the page number, and record the quotation or give a brief explanation of the event or section you will focus on, placing it in the context of the work.
2. Sketch a quick-draw that uses a symbol to indicate what your selection from the text *does* in the context of the story.
3. Add quotations from the section of text you are explicating to show how the event or quotation functions.
4. Write a claim, stating what your event or quotation does to contribute to the meaning of the whole.
5. Explain the graphic tie-in by developing an analogy between your symbol and the quotation or event. (e.g., not "I drew this wrapped

package because it answers all the remaining questions," but "Like a neatly wrapped package, the epilogue ties up all of the loose ends.")

It is important that students learn to recognize the difference between reporting an event and analyzing or interpreting it, a distinction which requires explicit teaching. We spend a good deal of class time generating a list of what an event or quotation can *do* to make meaning, and we continue to build this list throughout the year, distinguishing always between what the event is, or says, and what it does. Some questions that we consider are:

- Does it reveal something new about a character?
- Does it reinforce something about a character or a relationship?
- Does it add something to developing action?
- Does it introduce or develop an idea?
- Does it introduce a symbol or make reference to a symbol previously introduced?

Through such discussions, students learn about the structure of literature. They become aware of the strategies authors use, consciously or not, to make meaning. As they then work with these tools themselves, first in developing their cards and then in verbalizing and emulating the techniques, they become authors themselves, with an internal awareness of elements of the writer's craft. It is, of course, important to stress that a study of function is not an end in itself but a way to arrive more deeply at the central concern—the making of meaning.

Two additional examples illustrate the kind of thinking that interpretive cards, with their quick-draws, engender:

- Heidi Davis addressed a quotation from the end of the novel *My Antonia*, when Jim is walking through the fields outside of Black Hawk for the last time before returning to the East. "We possessed together the precious, the incommunicable past," Jim tells the reader. Heidi placed a bow in the center of her card, and wrote, "Like one wraps a present to pass on to someone else, this passage not only wraps up the story, it also wraps up Jim's memories of the past. It prepares him to look beyond his past to experience the present and finally to move on into his future."
- Linda Kim sketched a brick wall on the front of her card, to reflect Mr. Shimerda's eagerness for Antonia to learn English. "Te-e-ach, te-e-ach my Antonia!" Mr. Shimerda tells Jim at the beginning of the novel. Linda's interpretation of this event is as follows: "Antonia builds her determination to learn this new language to survive and to help her family to communicate with others. Not unlike the red bricks built up one by one, Antonia takes one step at a time to accomplish her goal of learning the English language."

The most basic way that students learn a new concept is to see that idea in terms of things that they already know, through the magic of metaphor. The quick-draw enables students to see how a portion of text functions by relating it to how something operates in their own lives. Through the drawing, students connect the familiar (the chameleon changing color to blend into the environment) to the unfamiliar (an event or symbol in a text that changes a character). As students examine the section of text they have chosen, they observe and analyze to determine its importance to the whole. They then clarify and validate their ideas as they imagine ways in which they can show its function visually. Through their writing, they explain *their* ideas in *their own* terms; they speak with the confidence and voice that comes from ownership of ideas and text.

THE QUICK-MAP

The quick-map is a technique that helps students clarify ideas visually. Sometimes students do quick-maps in pairs or groups during a portion of the class period; other times, they do them alone as homework. In either case, the construction of these maps is a generative process, serving as catalyst for class discussions and writing. They provide one more strategy in the students' continuing interaction with the text.

Often a quick-map assignment at the end of the first chapter of a novel will give students the mindset they need to understand the rest of the book. At the end of Chapter 1 of John Updike's *The Centaur*, for example, Advanced Placement students are often confused about the correspondences between the two levels of the story—the everyday reality of the story line and the mythical reality that parallels it. As an overnight homework assignment, they draw a quick-map to help them understand the relationships between George Caldwell and Chiron, Mr. Zimmerman and Zeus, Peter and Prometheus, and the rest of the inhabitants of Updike's real and mythical worlds. (See Figure 4–6 for an example.) This is often a difficult assignment for students; however, they all come to class (however apologetically) with *something* (they are, after all, AP students). As they share their ideas, using their quick-maps as a basis for group discussion, students immediately become aware of the wide range of valid responses that are available to this assignment. Not only does this diversity help them gain confidence in their own responses, it opens them up to the variations they see in the responses of others. Even the students who were most confused as they began this book are able to follow the interwoven strands of myth and reality as they continue to read.

In other books, a quick-map assignment can be useful in helping students understand complex, unfamiliar ideas as they arise. A difficult section of Joyce's *Portrait of the Artist as a Young Man* provides such an instance: When the class begins to cope with the theoretical conversation between Daedalus and his friend Lynch (cited in the Introduction to Part III), we stop and have them make a quick-map of the three stages in the apprehension of beauty that Stephen outlines. This is a class period or overnight assignment. For an example of one student's response, see Melissa LaFollette's study which appears as the frontispiece to Part III.

No two quick-maps of this section look anything alike; yet every student, in our experience, has been able to understand Joyce's description of how we apprehend beauty: first through seeing its *integritas*, its wholeness; then through analyzing the parts and seeing the *consonantia* or harmony they make in their different configurations; and finally through seeing the whole again, but this time with the *claritas* or radiance that comes from understanding the parts in relation to the whole. The students who do not immediately grasp the concept through an entirely individual process, come to understand it through the discussion that follows the sharing of graphics in class.

This technique, of stopping a work at a difficult point and asking students to attempt to represent the unfamiliar concept graphically, has implications for every subject matter. We think here of Einstein and Darwin who made their quantum leaps in relativity and evolution first visually, then, still carrying the images that prompted the illuminations, spent years validating them.

THE NOTETAKING MAP

When students read for content mastery, the notetaking map provides a method of organizing information spatially. It's especially adaptable to subjects which require the student to read and remember specific information—history and science, for example. To help students visualize the material for both immediate understanding and later review, we assign a quick-map, which enables them to organize information in a way that makes it visually accessible. For notetaking, we advise the use of contrasting colors or shapes to differentiate information received from the basic text, class discussion, and personal connections. Students begin the notetaking map by using *one color or shape* to identify key information from the textual assignment; they map this information visually to show the relative importance of items they include. As we discuss the material in class, students add ideas to their maps in a *second color or shape*. At any point in the process they may use a *third color or shape* to indicate related ideas from their own previous knowledge. Later, when reviewing this map, they have available at one glance notes stemming from a) the original text, b) the class discussion, and c) their own extensions. Not only does this visual map enhance their understanding of the text, it enables them to see how their own perceptions broaden and change as they hear and internalize the ideas of others.

Quick-maps make review time extremely efficient. By having chapters or sections of information mapped on single pages, students can see relationships that are often elusive when stretched out over pages of notes. The maps are not intended to supplant other kinds of notetaking, but should be thought of as one more alternative in the array of strategies designed to help students find their most efficient learning modes. (See Chapter 3 for definition and examples of the mapping process.)

This method of visual notetaking provides access to difficult information for all levels of students. We have found this technique extremely productive with our language-reluctant students, who are often able to process information visually before they can verbalize it. The quick-draws and quick-maps enable them to use a learning mode that is natural for them.

THE EVOLVING GRAPHIC

The evolving graphic can be an effective building tool as a class proceeds through a study of a work. The graphic can develop on the classroom wall as the class moves through a study of a work, a period, or a concept. During a study of Shakespeare's *Henry IV, Part I*, for instance, we put two life-sized figures on our wall on butcher paper (traced from two students who volunteered for the parts). One represented Prince Hal; the other, Hotspur, his foil. As we read through the play, each time we came to a reference that gave insight into either character, a student wrote it on the appropriate figure, with act, scene and line number, and with notes as to what the quotation indicated about the character.

Students really get involved in building these figures. They place their quotations on the figure thoughtfully rather than haphazardly, and use color very deliberately as they write on the figure. For instance, when Hotspur reacts impulsively, students place the quotation in his heart or viscera; they write quotations testifying to Hal's careful planning, however, in the appropriate lobe of his brain. Hotspur's figure almost immediately become filled with hot colors—reds, oranges, neon pinks; while Hal's remain cooler, though not pale, with shades of blue and green. In this way, the class builds impressions of their subject as they read—examining responses, modifying them, and drawing conclusions.

This process is effective in tracking changes, both of the reader's growing awareness of complexities in the work or of recurring or parallel elements in a text. A class might track parallel settings in a work (Belmont and Venice in *The Merchant of Venice,* for instance, or the forest and the town in *The Scarlet Letter*). A social studies class might build parallel graphics of two countries during a particular time period, or a science class might build graphics to represent the life stages of two different life forms. Such graphics give new life to the often-assigned comparison and contrast essay. In whatever classroom it is used, this evolving graphic process, as exemplified by Hal and Hotspur, intensifies and personalizes reading, enhances student understanding, and allows students to track and visualize progressive development.

Group graphics: Focusing on the parts

CHAPTER GRAPHICS

Graphics can be a vital part of an intensive study of a work after students have finished their first reading. Groups of students are assigned responsibility for chapters or sections of a work. Each group creates a graphic representative of the primary elements of their section as they discuss it in preparation for leading a discussion with the rest of the class. Students learn how to address issues of character, conflict, style, and idea through each chapter; to examine how each of the parts contributes to the meaning of the whole, and to make their study recursive, referring to previous chapters and chapter presentations as necessary to show how these elements develop.

Each group has these instructions: 1) Title the section. 2) Be responsible for knowing what happens in that section and how it relates to what comes before and after. 3) Construct a group graphic, which you will use in your presentation of your section to the class. This technique, illustrated in this section by *The Great Gatsby*, is easily adaptable to many works, and promotes intensive student-generated study of a work.

We divide the intensive work for the study of *The Great Gatsby* into nine working groups. After time for group graphic creation and discussion (for a substantive novel, this work may take a week of class time), each group assumes responsibility for presenting one chapter of the novel to the class. As each group of students presents, they put their graphic on the wall. The next group then links its presentation to elements that have been raised by the groups preceeding it. Students lead the discussion of the entire work, using their graphics to show both the relationships of elements within their chapter, and the progressive development of these elements throughout the novel.

The group that created Figure 4–7 focused their graphic on the masks that both Gatsby and Jordan presented to the world in the chapter they studied. Their quotations from the text, all chosen from this single chapter, reflect the surreal quality of how these characters appear to other characters as well as to the reader. In the class discussion, the group explained that they put cracks at the top and bottom, on each character's side, to show the fragility of the masks and to prepare us for the eventual revelation of the real characters.

Since all students have read the full work, these student-led presentations become full class discussions. Other students see connections to their own study and draw on them as they present their own sections of the book. All students in this way take full ownership of the class discussion and realize the work for themselves, rather than looking to the teacher to do it for them.

FROM GRAPHIC GROUPS TO WRITING GROUPS

After the group presentations, with the book now "graphed" on the wall, we restructure the graphic study groups to form writing response groups. Each writing group has at least one expert from each section of the book. These new groups function to help each student in the group define, explore, and expand on their ideas for their writing. If one student, for example, wants to trace the use of a color or symbol throughout a novel, each member of the group can talk authoritatively about how that symbol functions in one chapter. This kind of sharing, calling on individual expertise, provides breadth and depth to the student gathering ideas and data for a paper. This group, then, becomes the writing response group for the final paper, whether it is an interpretation, a reflective essay, or a series of poems.

GROUPS BASED ON LITERARY ELEMENTS

A short story or long poem also lends itself to group graphic study with a focus on specific literary elements within the whole work. Students may read and log their responses to Willa Cather's "Paul's Case," for example, before such a study. In this model, we divide students into four groups based on specific literary elements that we choose as appropriate to the study of the story: plot line, the character of Paul, symbol, and motif. The students use a class period to discuss their assigned literary element of the story, tracing it throughout, pulling quotations to validate their ideas. They sketch a symbol to reflect their ideas, and construct a graphic to show their perceptions of the development of that element through the story. Each group leads a discussion about the impact of the story as a whole, using as a pivot point their own study focus. Through this class discussion, they explore the interrelationships among all the parts and between the parts and the whole.

PRELUDE TO INTERPRETIVE WRITING

Although the graphic map can stand as an end in itself, it can also lead to a wide variety of writing assignments, ranging from the autobiographical to the interpretive; from the dramatic monologue to a poem. The *group graphic essay* is an effective way of teaching students to construct an interpretive paper using a short work that has a dominant focus. Students work on graphics in chapter or section groups to discover and formulate their ideas of how their section contributes to the overall dominant theme of the work. Because students are working with a small section of text, they do not become intimidated or lost and can focus their efforts on precision in constructing a thesis rather than on searching through pages for examples. The sharing of the group diffuses much of the "I can't write" syndrome as they work together to write a substantial interpretive paragraph. Because each group in the class is writing in response to the same general question, the parts, when viewed sequentially during presentations, often hold together to form an insightful and well-structured paper on the work as a whole.

Students see that the emergent paper has a direction established by group one; each subsequent section's paragraph sets up its premise, which is by the nature of the process linked to the overall question. In this way, during presentations, they are not only studying the work itself, they are studying the structure of an interpretive paper, watching the claims take shape and substance as each group presents its graphic essay to the class. Finally, when all sections are on the board, the class can work on transitions, smoothing the connections between sections, putting the finishing touches on their class interpretation.

Student work with Stephen Crane's short story "The Open Boat" provides an example of how this process works in the classroom. Students read through the story, which is divided into seven parts, and respond to it individually in writing before any discussion takes place. Then, each section group assumes responsibility for looking closely at one section of the story. Students construct a graphic to show how their particular section of the story contributes to the meaning and impact of the whole.

The groups work first from their individual responses to the section, then integrate these to form specific claims about their particular section of the text. This process requires a very close examination of how that section functions within the framework of the whole—how it contributes to the development of the character, the mood, the ideas, and the style of the story. After completing a first reading and response to the story, the groups have the benefit of retrospect in collecting their thoughts and planning their graphics. As in constructing the interpretive cards, students decide on a central symbol to reflect their section and incorporate quotations and events in the text to validate their ideas. Students in each small group work together to write a short interpretation of their section. This process enables them first to *see* their section in the context of the whole, and then to state and validate concrete claims about how their part contributes to the meaning of the whole.

The group studying section six of Stephen Crane's "The Open Boat" incorporated the symbol of the fly from their graphic (shown in Figure 4–8) into their interpretive section. Their contribution to the group essay follows:

The death of a mere fly is rather insignificant in our daily lives, and it is because of this that a dead fly symbolizes section 6 of Stephen Crane's short story "The Open Boat". It is in this section that the correspondent ponders a death he feels will be his eventual fate—a death that will go as unnoticed as the death of a fly. It is at this point, when faced with death, that the correspondent remembers a time when the death of a human life meant nothing to him. Similarly, we can only feel for the death of a fly when we too have faced a similar situation. If we were never faced with death, we would have no sense of remorse or sadness for the fly. Not knowing the pain or sadness it might feel, its death would not have a great impact on our lives. Here again a connection between the fly and the correspondent can be made, since, just as the loss of a fly means nothing to us, the correspondent realizes that an impartial Nature will feel nothing about his death. The helplessness of the men is acute in this section, as they lay victim to whatever the future has in store. All they can do is watch and wait, and know that, in the large scene of things, nature cares as little for them as they do for the fly.

This section, placed in context with the interpretive writings from the other groups, adds to the group essay, a valuable adjunct to other approaches to teaching interpretation. We generally find a student who will print up a copy of the whole for class distribution. The fact that students want their group writing in their writing folders attests to their involvement in the project.

Examining the whole

We begin with the whole and move to a study of the parts. Unlike the zoologist, who must leave the fragments of the frog on the preparation tray, we can then return to the whole, integrating the parts, reforming and informing our sense of the whole—poem, work, thematic unit, course. In this phase of our study, graphics have an important role to play.

STUDY OF A COMPLETE WORK

In graphics projects based on a complete work—novel, play, short story—
students draw ideas and examples from the whole rather than from any
individual part. Students might examine the organizational structure of a
work: is it episodic in nature, like Steinbeck's *Cannery Row*; does it detail
ramifications of a single event on a character's life, as in *The Pearl*; or
does it depend on the effects of a particular story-telling technique such
as the flashback in *A Separate Peace*? Students might integrate a number
of the major motifs, or construct a plot map to show the sequence of
events. These graphics might be entirely verbal maps; they might include
both symbols and words; or they might be wholly conceptual. This
technique of constructing a graphic map after the class has had some
discussion of the work enables students to return yet again to the text, to
collect their thoughts about the work as a whole, and to explore
relationships among its various elements—structure, style, plot, character,
symbol, theme.

For second language students, and for students who may have trouble
understanding the plot line of a story, the creation of an overview graphic
allows them to clarify questions they might have at a literal level so that
they can move on to the more abstract levels of comprehension. Often
students can't pinpoint the sources of their confusion; they only know
they're confused, and so are hit with the frustration of their confusion and
of their own inability to be clear enough even to formulate a question. As
students move through the graphic process, they learn precisely where
their understanding breaks down—at the point where they can no longer
conceptualize what's happening. The act of mapping, showing
relationships graphically, helps take them through the point of confusion
to clarity.

Students find mapping a useful tool in enabling them to see the
connections that link the disparate parts of a work. Through this process
they are able to see how characters are shaped by events, and how, in
turn, the events are shaped by the characters. They are able to track ideas
and symbols through the work, and to discover the relationships among
characters, events, ideas, and techniques. Judi Rich's graphic "The World
According to Salinger" (Figure 4–9) shows the connections that link the
diverse elements of the work, in this case, the nine stories.

Judi depicts the relationships among Salinger's characters in *Nine
Stories* by using a telephone cord as her unifying symbol. Her
understanding of the personalities of each character shows clearly through
the stylized drawings and her grasp of the connections among them is
evidenced by the quotations she chooses—by who is saying what to
whom. As she connects the characters with the phone cord, she conveys
the logical connections among the characters visually. Judi lets us see
these characters as she sees them on the phone—the positions they are
in, the tones they use. While presenting her graphic to the class, she
clearly articulates her ideas about Salinger's tone—the caustic, satiric
voice that underlies and connects all nine stories.

THE GRAPHIC TIMELINE

The graphic timeline provides students with a firm sense of narrative. Students create a timeline, highlighting critical events, and choosing symbols and colors to reflect their choices. (See Figure 4–10 for an example.) It is the purposeful incorporation of symbols and color that enables students to move from a summary of events to discussion and writing about ideas. This activity, done individually or in pairs, promotes a close re-reading and analysis as students choose pivotal events and determine why each is significant. Both the selection process and the sketching of symbols brings students to a deeper understanding of how the events of the work are interrelated with character and idea development.

Even in graphing a timeline, not all events will appear on all timelines; students select events based on their individual perception. As with all reader response activities, students' own experiences govern how they perceive what they read. Group and class discussions of individual graphics add to everyone's ability to see a work from multiple points of view. Following the suggestions for the notetaking map presented earlier in this chapter—different colors or shapes to indicate material from different sources, you might want to give students the option of adding events introduced by other students to their individual timelines.

VERBAL AND CONCEPTUAL GRAPHICS

Graphics can help students synthesize their understanding of wide-ranging aspects of a work, from its structure and character relationships to recurring images and themes. Whether totally verbal, as in Figure 4–11, totally conceptual, as in Figure 4–12, or a combination of words and symbols, these graphics give an overview of the students' perceptions of a whole work. They enable students to connect and clarify their ideas about the literature, discovering and revising meaning as they go through the graphic process, and solidifying their perceptions as they articulate their ideas in both oral and written presentations.

Maxine Leong approaches John Updike's *The Centaur* by chapters, examining various elements of the novel in each of the nine chapters, using separate colors to show the connections between the mythical and contemporary realities. She uses the graphic process to integrate the structure, character, and mythic counterparts in the novel.

The conceptual graphic illustrated in Figure 4–12 presents a student's insight into how structure and meaning are interrelated and interdependent in such a work as biologist Lyall Watson's novel *Gifts of Unknown Things*.

In this conceptual graphic, Jeannette Hudson shows her understanding of the structure of the novel by integrating the four divisions of the book—air, earth, fire, and water—into her graphic. Linking the young girl, who is the focal point of the novel, to the four elements, Jeannette makes the girl's sensory knowledge of the world explicit. This conceptual graphic presents the student's sophisticated understanding of the way structure and meaning coalesce in this novel.

One of the exciting results of using graphics is seeing the wide range of responses to a single assignment. Once students have internalized the various kinds of graphics, they mix, match, combine, and otherwise extend the possibilities far beyond our original vision. Figures 4–13 and 4–14 show how two students translated a single assignment—to design a graphic showing the relationship of ideas in Galsworthy's *The Apple Tree* and Keats' "Ode on a Grecian Urn"—into their own purposes.

These two approaches to the assignment explore the basic dualities that underlie both works. The students—one through symbols, the other through words—explore the dualities they find in these works as they examine such issues as fantasy and reality, stasis and change, impulsive actions (the Dionysian element), and logical reasoning (the Apollonian).

Because students begin with personal responses and test their ideas throughout the interplay of language and art, they produce graphics that reflect their own unique perceptions. The cumulative class effect can be dramatic; as each student or group of students shares perceptions, the entire class begins to see things from different perspectives, developing not only a deeper awareness of the text or idea itself, but becoming more aware of number of vantage points from which any single idea or work can be approached. This process, augmented by each student's final paper, brings students to a realization of the breadth and depth of literature, enabling them to see why some works persist and ideas recur, crossing both time and geographic barriers. When they do see images that a number of them share for the same work, they begin to internalize a real understanding of the concept of archetype, whether they know the word or not. The graphics, then, serve both to endorse their own sense of uniqueness and to enhance their sense of belonging.

This drawing shows an ant carrying an apple, looking up at some large stairs.
Even though he thinks he can't climb them, he is going to try. This
represents Atticus defending Tom Robinson even though he knows he will lose.

4-1 Quick-Draw: *To Kill a Mockingbird* by Matt Ackerman

Sudden emotion is like a storm. If one's prepared for it, he might be able to
retreat to a house or some type of shelter, as Hester, to avoid it. If,
however, one is unprepared, like the man, the deluge will engulf him and he'll
definitely become soaked.

4-2 Quick-Draw: *The Scarlet Letter* by Kirby Lawton

This graphic represents the result of greed. The man is devoid of color
because it is a representation of his soul as it is corrupted away. He puts
all of his faith in material things instead of other people. He looks to the
pearl to see the future. The future then becomes a crystal ball. Wispy
images float across it as he intently watches. His greed leads to distrust,
then to paranoia, as his soul disappears. He locks it away, clasping it with
all his might.

4-3 Quick-Draw: *The Pearl* by David Kiewlich

Antonia moves from her rough
farm life to live with the
Harlings in town.

(pg.113) "the Harlings' house seemed, as she said,
'like Heaven' to her. She was never too tired to
make taffy or chocolate cookies for us."
(pg.80) " ' I can work like a mans now...' "
(pg.81) " Antonia ate so noisily now, like a man..."
(Pg.100) - ' The girl will be happy here, and she'll forget
those things,' said Mrs. Harling. "

4-4A "The Chameleon" by Julia Ng (Front View)

With a change of environment,
Antonia transforms from the masculine
farmworker to a more feminine girl.
Like a chameleon, Antonia's character-
is affected by her surroundings. Her
move marks a change in personality
through the influences of city life.

4-4B "The Chameleon" by Julia Ng (Back View)

p. 199 On a muddy March day, Antonia sets out from her home to take the night train to Denver, where she will marry Larry Donovan.

" 'It was in March, if I remember rightly, and a terrible muddy, raw spell, with the roads bad for hauling her things to town ... 'Twas a cold, raw day he drove her and her three trunks into Black Hawk to take the night train for Denver.' " p. 199

The conditions which Antonia faces as she leaves her home to start her new life as a married woman foreshadows what her marriage holds for her.

4-5A Interpretive Card by Rowena Ng (Front View)

Like the crystal ball, the conditions surrounding Antonia's departure from Black Hawk fortells what her future marriage will be like. Instead of leaving her home and friends in the joyous blessing of a sunny spring day, she leaves on a cold, muddy, raw day to take a night train to her new home. Her environment does not forebode well for her new married life.

4-5B Interpretive Card by Rowena Ng (Back View)

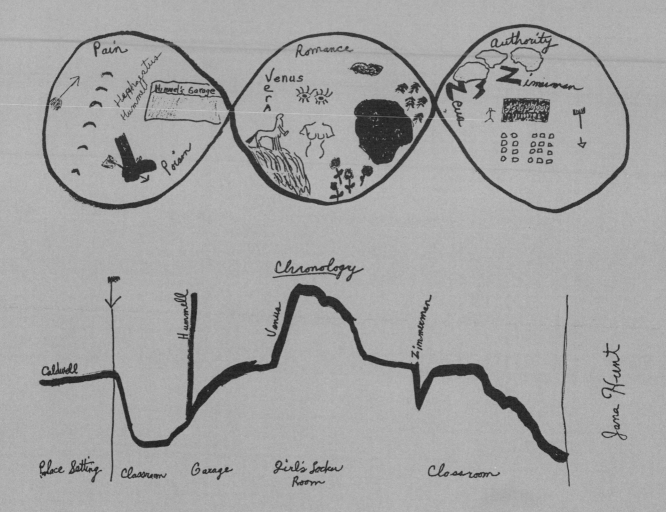

4-6 Quick Map of chapter from *The Centaur* by Jana Hunt

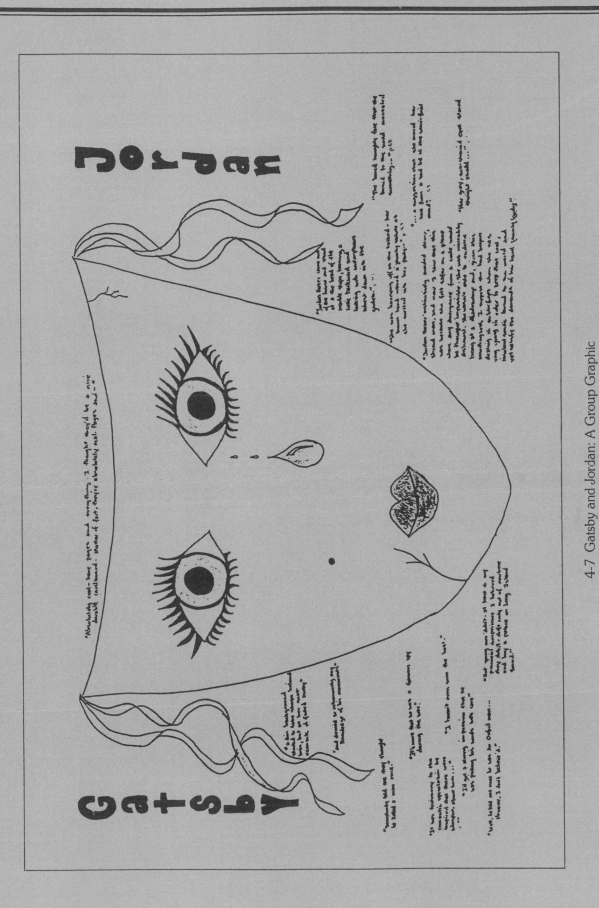

4-7 Gatsby and Jordan: A Group Graphic

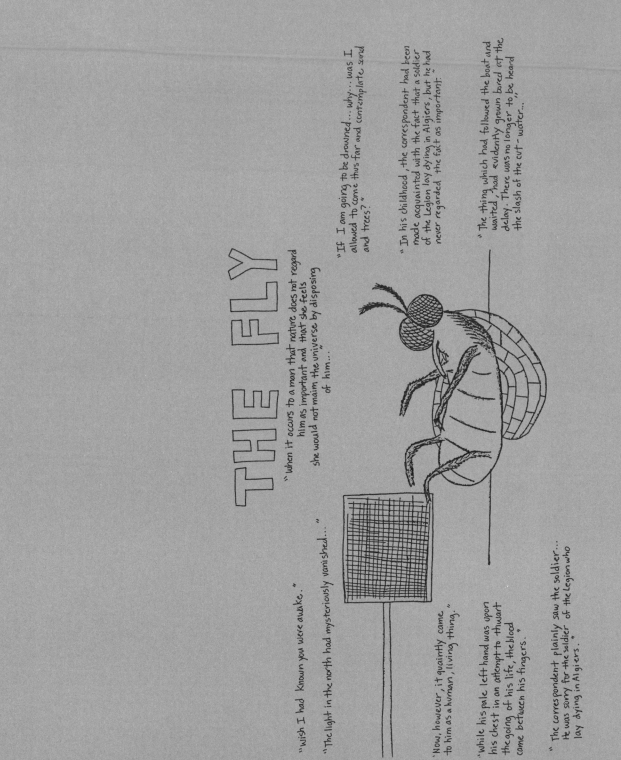

THE FLY

"When it occurs to a man that nature does not regard him as important and that she feels she would not maim the universe by disposing of him...."

"wish I had known you were awake."

"The light in the north had mysteriously vanished...."

"Now, however, it quaintly came to him as a human, living thing."

"while his pale left hand was upon his chest in an attempt to thwart the going of his life, the blood came between his fingers."

"The correspondent plainly saw the soldier.... He was sorry for the soldier of the Legion who lay dying in Algiers."

"If I am going to be drowned...why...was I allowed to come thus far and contemplate sand and trees?"

"In his childhood, the correspondent had been made acquainted with the fact that a soldier of the Legion lay dying in Algiers, but he had never regarded the fact as important."

"The thing which had followed the boat and waited, had evidently grown bored at the delay. There was no longer to be heard the slash of the cut-water...."

4-8 Drawing from group study of "The Open Boat"

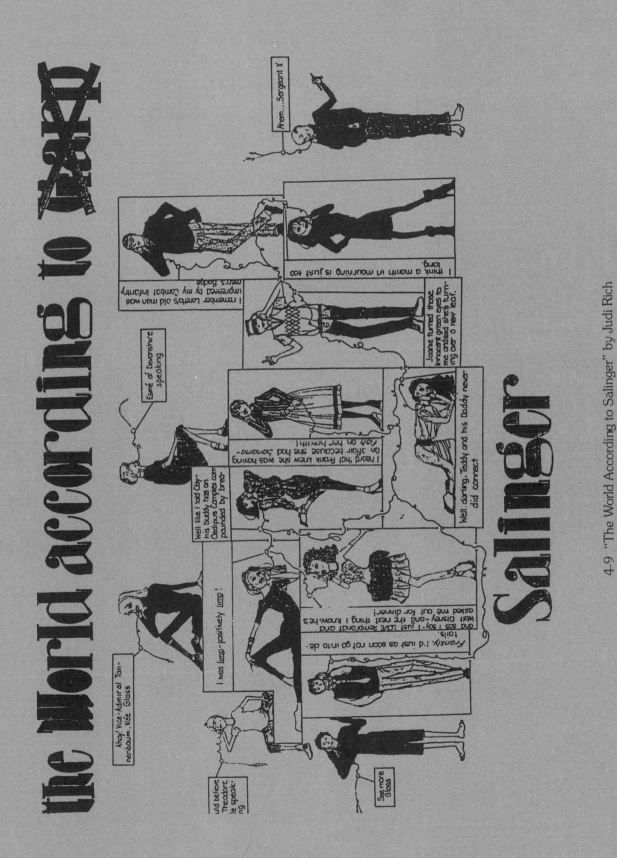

4-9 "The World According to Salinger" by Judi Rich

4-10   Timeline of *The Call of the Wild* by Elizabeth Fields

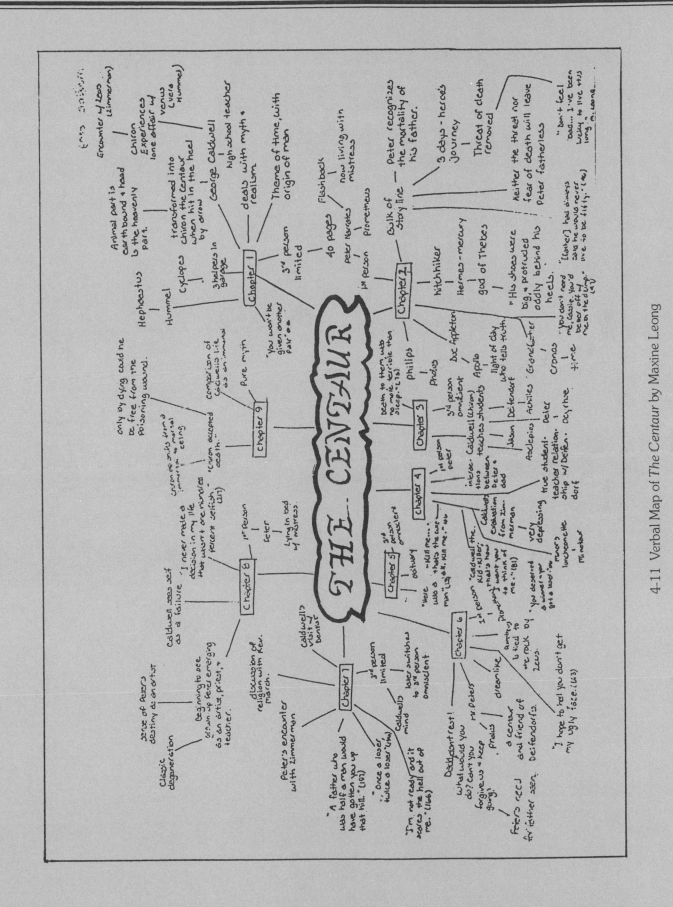

4-11 Verbal Map of *The Centaur* by Maxine Leong

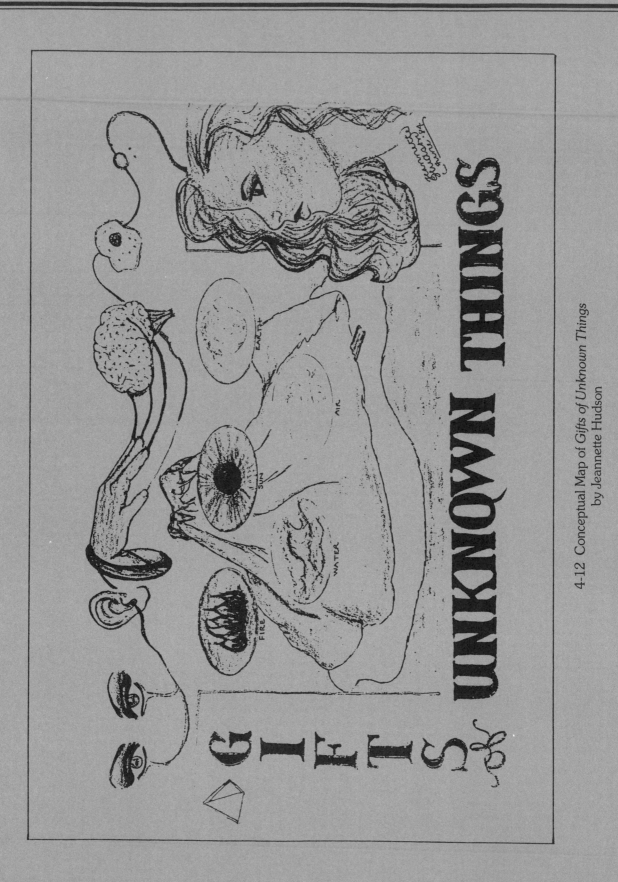

4-12 Conceptual Map of *Gifts of Unknown Things*
by Jeannette Hudson

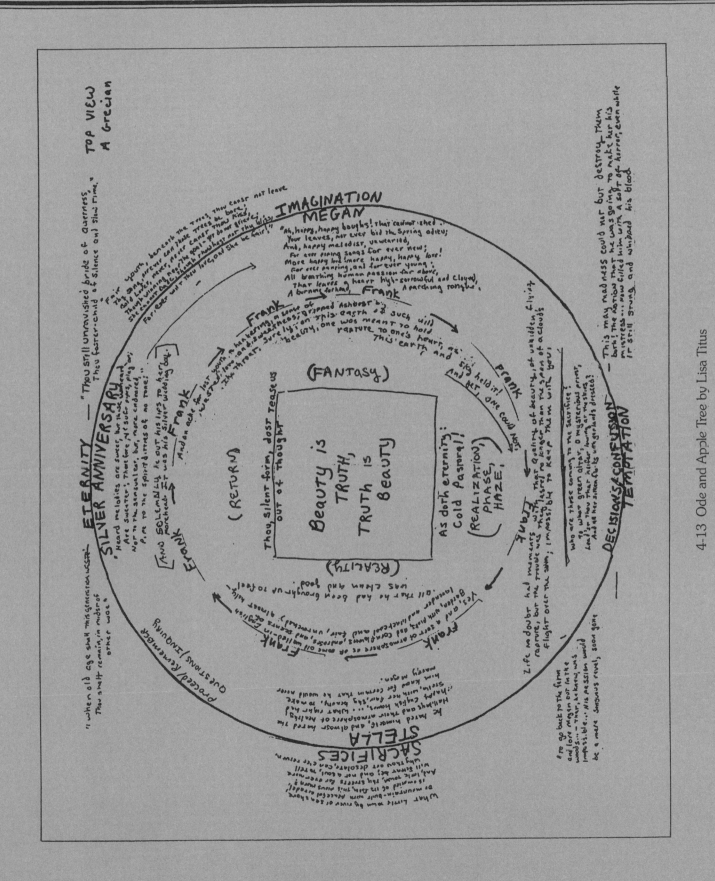

4-13 Ode and Apple Tree by Lisa Titus

4-14 Ode and Apple Tree by Carl Bird

CHAPTER 5

EXTENDED APPLICATIONS: PAGES OF POSSIBILITIES

It is never the thing,
but the version of the thing.

WALLACE STEVENS

The possibilities for extending metaphoric thinking and graphics reach into every discipline. We're going to focus here, however, on using graphics in writing that arises from personal experience and in the ongoing classroom assessment that is one of our many realities.

Graphic catalysts for personal writing

The quick-draws and extended metaphors which we often use as a part of reading logs (see Chapter 4), can also be used, independently of literature, as catalysts for personal writing. These techniques, which ask students to make both verbal and graphic metaphors that freeze-frame a moment, an object, or a situation, are valuable pre-writing techniques that lead students quite naturally into poetry or prose.

WRITING ABOUT A PERSON OR EVENT: THE BIOGRAPHICAL SKETCH

A one-period warm-up exercise for writing about a person uses a quick-draw, along with some suggestions for helping students define their subjects. We begin with a short, informal visualization (see Chapter 1 for extended mandala visualization techniques) in which students create metaphors both for their subject and for themselves:

Imagine that you are looking at the person you are going to write about. See the person physically—the height, the shape of the body, facial expression, clothes. Hear the voice, experiencing its texture and its tenor as the person speaks, and observe your own reactions as the person speaks. Bring the person sharply into your mind's eye. What kind of animal is this person most like? Imagine this person with the qualities of the animal you have chosen. In relation to this person, what kind of animal do you become? Try to see these two "sun-animals" in some relation to each other. Is one dominant? Are they naturally compatible? Incompatible? Think for a moment about how these animals interact in the natural world.

Coming back to this person and yourself as human beings, remember a time when you were both in the same place or same situation. Visualize this person in a particular instance with you—a time when your subject in some way reflects the animal image you chose earlier. See the person in his or her relationship to you within the framework of your event. Now run a filmstrip of the event in your mind's eye. See all the details—the interaction, the actions, the speech; observe the sun-animal qualities that emerged in this event.

This visualization takes about ten minutes. Students then, without talking or sharing, do a quick-draw of the incident they visualized, capturing the relative positions of the other person and of themselves at one moment of the event. We don't need to ask them to choose and draw one moment of the event; by simply sketching it, they automatically freeze-frame a moment. The act of drawing naturally focuses their attention on the pivotal moment in the incident.

It is this pivotal event, the essence of an incident, that becomes the basis for a piece of either poetry or prose. We encourage students in this exercise to write in the present and to replay the event in writing as they played it in their minds, bringing in references to their animal metaphors if they seem appropriate. For students who need a structural starting point for this writing exercise, we suggest that they begin a series of stanzas or paragraphs with "I see you. . .," and build a succession of images from their sketches and first drafts. This process (visualization, quick-draw, first draft writing) takes less than one class period. As homework, then, or during class the next day, they complete their poems or short prose pieces.

Although students' first drafts for this exercise are often written in prose, many students turn to poetry to fine tune their visualizations. Poems that emerge are both personal and metaphoric, as students naturally weave their metaphors and their encounter with the subject of their visualization together. In the first example, Jana Hunt uses the image of scars as "three white blotches shaped like the Great Lakes" to focus the incident she recalled during the visualization.

RIGHT NOW THEY'RE INVISIBLE

White hidden in whiteness,
like the famous picture of the white cow
eating marshmallows in a snow storm
that children talk about,
but when summer comes
and my skin begins to tan,
they will appear like secret messages
written in invisible ink by a Russian spy.

When I look at these three white blotches
shaped like the Great Lakes on my elbow,
I see myself standing
on tip-toe
struggling to reach the counter-top
that was then six inches
above my head.

I see my fingers
grasping for the cookies
placed purposely beyond my reach,
and instead catching hold of the cord,
and screaming as coffee grounds
and black pools of water splattered
and splashed, and my mother,
her make-up half on and her hair
in rollers, running in and
"Why can't you be more careful?
... like a bull in a china shop...."
Then she saw I was crying, and the blood,
and held my elbow under the faucet
letting the cool water wash over it,
apologizing over and over, and I cried
as I watched the red skin blister,
not knowing that the sun
would one day make me remember
how it felt to be small.

JANA HUNT

Advanced Placement students are usually highly proficient in writing interpretive and evaluative essays, but they often feel inadequate when it comes to writing poetry unless teachers value it, making poetry as much a part of the curriculum as analysis. Since value is often equated with allotted time, we do provide time for students to learn to write poetry. We believe strongly in the power of the poem as a way of enabling students to deal with primary issues—metaphor, precision of diction, structure—as well as with expression of feelings and ideas. It seems ironic that teachers of college-bound students so often diminish curricular possibilities by teaching the analysis but not the creation of both narrative fiction and poetry.

The following two poems, written by Advanced Placement seniors, make use of extended animal metaphors. In their sketches, students depict incidents in which they put themselves into some relationship with the metaphoric animal. The resulting poems show the connections that arise from the initial metaphor, and the specific focus on incident that the quick-draw elicits.

TARANTULA

Soft and furry
The tarantula crawled quietly
Along the table toward me.
I wanted to take him home with me,
Child that I was.

How could anyone think
You could hurt a fly
Or kill a man after you stepped by
With your soft legs.

That man held you and made me jealous.
I wanted to touch you
First, wanted to feel your power.

Something inside me told me to beware,
Kept me from the fatal grab.
The spider would not be possessed
Ever. Only a fool would try.

Now the spider crawls into my life again.
He sneaks into my brain, my heart
So coyly, his furry paws tickling me.
Hidden in him lies the death I feared before.
Afraid again deep inside, I will not be seduced
Until I too have a weapon.

Lover, with your soft arms and legs
You taunt me like a tarantula taunts a fly.
Am I your fly? or am I only a web
You will discard when I am old?
I am dying to know.

BY CHRIS WALTON

WHITE SWAN

The clear pool ripples silently,
mimicking my movements. I have no
bearings, floating effortlessly like
a ball of cotton, white and full,
suspended on the water's surface.

Ahead, near the shore, droplets of
water spatter about as a duck
pointlessly flaps his wings.

Now the glare from the sun becomes
bright. I dip my neck and head
into the cool blueness. In the shade
a green fern wavers in the breeze.

A red bill, but here black feathers
frame it. Black; moments before,
white. I quickly immerse my whole
body under water, staying there as
long as I can. Finally I swim up.

I look straight at a wet rock that
sits in the center of the pond. From
under it comes a black swan, in the
place where I once was.

ANNICK MEBINE

THE COMPUTER MAP

So many students have access to computers either at school or at home that we find computer-drawn maps appearing more and more frequently. We were particularly interested in the way one student wrote up a childhood memory: after sketching an initial map on his computer about a field trip to Yosemite with his fifth grade class (Figure 5–1), Arvind Rao wrote up a rough first draft of his memory. His writing response group prodded him to recall further details, which he did in a second-draft computer map before revising his writing (Figure 5–2). The resulting piece, which is too long to print here, is rich with the kind of detail that emerges from the combined acts of sketching (by computer or by hand), drafting, working with a response group, revising the map, then revising the writing.

The graphic-interview connection

The interview has become an integral part of our everyday lives: radio, television, newspaper, magazine—the media depend on interviews. Students are commonly assigned interviews in many subjects in school— an interview with a civic leader in history; an investigative report for science or social science; a family history interview in English; and, of course, interviews for the school newspaper. Graphics can be used in several ways to help students develop interviewing techniques that will allow them to be both astute critics of press interviews and effective presenters of their own subjects.

After several days of preliminary interview work—reading interviews, trying out questions on classmates, conducting practice interviews in class, deciding on the subject for the interview, setting up the date, place, and time—students are ready for the actual interview. We encourage students to sketch the setting of the interview as quickly as possible following the meeting. In this sketch, students try to capture background elements to use later in their writing. As part of the interview preparation, we discuss the value of location in revealing a person's tastes and interests. A quick-draw of a room or office can be invaluable later on.

Students also sketch their impressions of their subjects; they find the mandala categories useful as a way into the relaxed discussion they want for the interview. Many students turn the mandala format around and ask their subjects to come up with the metaphors. "What animal do you think you are most like?" becomes one way for students to open up the conversation. Followed up with color or number, the discussion is on its way.

After students complete an interview, and that may mean more than one visit, students use notes, sketches, and memories to map essential facts and ideas they want to capture in their written interviews. Students use the map to organize their sketches, impressions, notes, and metaphorical images in preparation for their written interviews. The interviews themselves often sound highly professional, drawing as they do on meticulous observation, imagery, direct quotations, and thoughtful reflection. Figure 5–3 shows a graphic interview map in the shape of a cross, appropriate as the subject of the interview is the student's pastor.

Reshma Patel, a junior, uses both the mandala categories and the mapping process in synthesizing her impressions of an interview with her father (Figure 5–4). She uses the mandala exercise to focus the metaphorical images she gained from her interview; and she uses the mapping process to integrate these images into her factual observations.

Here are some of the extended metaphors that Reshma created for her father:

An ivy plant grows rapidly and crawls into every crevice and crack. My father likes to get things done fast, and everything he does has to be finished to the end. He doesn't leave any room for anything to go wrong in anything he does.

The animal my father reminds me of is a porcupine because one really has to step lightly around him. One has to be very careful not to get him angry, because he gets very prickly when he loses his temper.

My father may be prickly on the outside, but inside I think he's soft, like a teddy bear. He doesn't show his feelings to other people, and he hides what he feels, so people won't see his weaknesses.

Reshma's resulting written interview is a perceptive study characterized by a richness of language and understanding, reflecting her own growth in understanding her father.

In one assignment—a study of the immigrant experience evolving out of the study of Cather's *My Antonia*—students interview a member of the community who has immigrated to the United States. After the interview, they fill out a sun-shadow mandala chart, then write sun sentences to describe the person they have interviewed. Julia Ng, a junior, interviewed her mother; here are several of her sun-sentences:

Like a cube, she is balanced and precise, planted stable on the ground.

She is like the classical luster of gold, bringing out traditions with a shimmer to befit the modern society.

She is the number two, with a base firmly planted, but turning and curving to look both inward and back.

She is a period, final and self-assured, confident of where she belongs.

Students draw mandalas from their sun-shadow charts, then write poems about the subject before, finally, writing up the interview itself. These final written interviews are rich in detail and imagery, reflecting the students' total involvement with the subjects.

For many students, this process is particularly moving as they frequently interview one of their parents or other family members; the experience brings them to a new understanding of themselves, their interview subject, and of the many conflicting emotions that life can hold for an immigrant in America.

The following piece, written by Julia Ng, reflects the new understanding she gains of her mother, an understanding that emerges first through her interview and mandala (see Figure 5–5), crystallizes as she creates her poem, and culminates in the following piece.

LOOKING FOR MY MOTHER

In the summer, she would wake up moist under the smoldering Philippine sun. Her youth was spent amid the paved but broken roads of Paco, a district of Manila, with the rundown buses raising the heavy dust thick into the air. She saw her home, as she saw all of the Philippines: a poor, broken, hot place. She was a girl who knew the heat well, for each day she worked and sweated in it, along with all that radiated from the hot ovens of her family's bakery. Yes, heat and hard work were two things she was well acquainted with. They both wore her down, yet made her resilient. She grew up out of that heat, the broken roads, the dust; she became a strong, enduring woman before she moved from the Philippines. She became a woman of stamina, vitality, courage, yearning. She became all these things, before she moved to America, and became my mother.

Her past seems so foreign to me, that when she speaks of it, I picture someone else instead of my mother. I see a young woman, strong and vibrant, the one that always smiles crooked in the black and white photos. She was one who always looked a bit bashful and nervous; dark glasses sometimes hide her eyes. I form this image as I hear my mother's voice carving out the figure and I see her as I examine the faded pictures that spill out from her old and dusty shoebox.

Julia goes on to detail, through anecdotes, her mother's arrival in America, and the difficulties she faced as she worked to make a home in a new culture. Through the entire interview, Julia's own sense of self-discovery emerges strongly and clearly. This process was truly generative, bringing Julia to a new understanding of both herself and her mother. Toward the end of the piece she tells us,

She [Julia's mother] was laconic and quiet when she spoke of leaving her parents behind to enter into a new country with a new husband. I was unearthing old memories with my questions, and I could see the effect of sad, hard remembrances on her face. She nodded while she spoke, tightened her lips. Her eyes concentrated on something in the far off distance and would rarely meet my own. Then the questioning suddenly ceased.

I watched her quick hands straighten out the photos on the table in a neat, rectangular pile. She stopped for a moment, and stared at a picture of a young girl, dressed in a white dress. Her hair was pulled back in pins and her dress hung loosely, billowing in the wind, as she stood on some steps.

I would never know this girl. I would never connect her with my mother. To me, she would always be a separate person, no matter how hard I tried to see her as my mother. This girl's hair was longer, more stringy, as if the moisture in the air was clinging to it. My mother's hair is neatly permed and cropped to frame her face. This girl's skin was flushed and smooth. My mother's face is dry with powder and foundation, little crevices edging their way around her eyes. The two pair of eyes stare back at me, both saying the same thing: the past belongs to them, and though I can sift through the hundreds of photographs and listen to the echoed memories, I will never even begin to understand.

Using graphics as part of the assessment process

AN END OF UNIT ASSIGNMENT

"Choose one of the three options below and map your ideas as the basis for a final essay for this unit. You may use books, notes, people, and any other resources you wish."

So begins a final assignment on Steinbeck for a class of juniors who have read *The Grapes of Wrath*, reread *Of Mice and Men* from their sophomore year, and read one additional work in groups. The three options pose a range of Steinbeck-related writing activities, but each requires a firm grounding in his work. Students are not threatened by this exam; they have read and logged their responses to the books; engaged in small group discussions and the making of chapter or whole book graphics; written a number of short pieces about the characters and ideas—they know what they feel and think about the importance of Steinbeck's work. Some of them have been to visit Steinbeck's home in Salinas, California, making a video of their trip to share with the class. Others have presented an interview in which all of Steinbeck's responses have been culled from his letters. Although their logs have been done individually, much of their work has been collaborative; now, however, they are completely comfortable taking the responsibility for their own writing, knowing that this final essay, while important, is only one of many indications the teacher has of their understanding of the work for the Steinbeck unit.

Lee Seale chose to use the form of a typical Steinbeck chapter in which an extended metaphor serves as a transition or interlude between narrative chapters:

It's a cool day. In a large forest on a huge mountain lies a small rock. If you looked closely at the rock, you would see a tiny sparkle. A small drop of water sits on the rock. Alone. No real direction. The hot sun sucks the vitality out of the water. It diminishes in size—almost gone. Completely at the mercy of nature—no control.

Nearby, another drop gathers. Augmented by additional drops, it gathers and the weight of it increases until it is capable of flowing down the side of the rock. As it does so, it passes over the nearly gone, lone drop. Now they are one. Flowing, picking up more stray drops as it gathers speed, it leaves a shiny trail of the lost. Remnants of those who didn't make it.

But the rest move on. Now a sturdy trickle, its size and speed increase. But if the distance to travel is too long, the trickle will wear dangerously thin. Then it will be incapable of movement. Fragmented and shallow, its vitality will be gone. It will sit, victim of the elements, and reduce. Dust will gather on it. Sun and heat will dry it up. Wind spreads it even thinner. Then it will no longer be water. Chemically broken down, it is now one with the earth. Almost like a man six feet under.

But our drops move on. It searches, as a group, to find hospitable conditions in which it can flourish—possibly a cool, shady piece of earth where it can join with others to make a pond, each supporting one another in a favorable environment.

But our trickle doesn't settle yet. That is okay. It is joined with others and increased in numbers. Now a stream, it has force. It is the controller, now. Its enemies, such as dust, succumb to its will. The momentum gathers. It cuts through the earth, shaping its paths to accommodate its needs.

It continues to pick up stray drops. Unable to support themselves, the community of water supports them. Taking what it needs, giving what it has. A flourishing river. There is power in numbers. One cannot do alone what many can do together.

When conditions get bad, the river fragments. Groups take alternative routes. Some find better conditions of survival. Some even find larger bodies of water to group with. Yet, for most, splitting means weakening. The tributary loses speed. Loses force. Loses control. No longer the shaper of its destiny, the drop submits to the will of the earth. Like a man all alone.

For this end of unit exam, the final grade is based on the graphic (specifically the way in which the graphic gives shape and substance to the writing), the student presentation, the written work, and the student's self-evaluation.

REDUCING THE PAPER LOAD

Graphics can substantially cut down on the paper load while serving as a valuable index to learning: a quick-map before reading a new work may serve as an introduction to a topic and let us know who knows what about myth, for example. A quick-draw serves as a daily reading check; a quick-map identifies areas of difficulty in a particular reading assignment. Thirty of these brief sketches or maps can be assessed in a quarter of the time it would take to read papers written in ten minutes. With a maximum of three points for these overnight or short in-class assignments, it takes just a few minutes to record a number in the gradebook. We keep all of these short assignment grades together and have an immediate picture of the day-to-day participation of all of our students.

We have another kind of picture always before us—the testimony of the walls as an indicator of student involvement and understanding. One of the spinoffs from using graphics in our classrooms is that we never have to design a bulletin board. Within a week or two after the beginning of the school year, our walls are brightly-colored collages of student work, graphically representing the students themselves, the books which they are studying, the poems and essays which they are writing. Every student who meets in that room can claim some part of those walls. Ownership implies investment and subtly affects the attitudes of students entering that room. We used to arrange all of their work on the walls ourselves, but soon came to see that student ownership of their room includes putting their own work up, often as they explain it to the rest of the class. Our only problem has been the lack of wall space to contain the graphics of the five or six classes that meet in our rooms. (Yes, we have to share rooms and walls, too. And now that all the teachers in our department use graphics, we really do run short of wall space.) These walls provide an ongoing assessment for the students as well as for us.

STUDENT SELF-EVALUATION

Although we are constantly assessing student work in the classroom in a variety of ways, we use graphics very specifically as a means of assessing individual learning. In our standard end-of-course project, which integrates graphics, presentations, and writing, students first have the task of integrating ideas and works from an entire semester into a single graphic. They begin by preparing a portfolio of the work that, for them, represents their experience in the class. Their final graphic is accompanied by writing; they may choose the form of their writing and often include both poems and interpretive papers. The final aspect of the portfolio is a paper in which students attempt to evaluate their own participation in the class and their growth during the course. They discuss, too, how the ideas they have coped with during the course have altered or extended their thinking about what is really important to them.

To illustrate the power of reflective self-evaluation, we include a partial transcript of Billy Tsai's presentation, along with a description of how he integrated the graphic into his discussion.

This year we have been exposed to many genres of literature, but what I have really come to recognize is that as we have studied these works we learn much more about ourselves. As I look back to the notes and annotations in the works, there are certain ideas that immediately strike me. By understanding and seeing what values I hold inside, it has become much easier for me to identify with myself—to develop a true understanding of who I am and who I want to be.

As I reflected on the works we had read this year, to put together my project, I pulled out what I had annotated to see what was important in the works, and more important, to see what was important to me. So much of what we read and talked about in here is a reflection of what I think and who I am, and so, in a way, I guess I am also a reflection of what we've read and talked about. Mirror images work both ways.

Billy then proceeded to use his old logs and graphics to share with the class some of his own reflections about individual works and ideas we had addressed. Citing *My Antonia*, *Catcher in the Rye*, Thoreau, *The Odyssey* and a number of other pieces, including poetry, he said,

Much of my own writing in response to what we were reading explored my childhood. The fact that I was very much affected by these books made me understand how very tied to my homeland I am—how very deep my roots have been. I'd never quite realized this until I saw these works and realized their effect on me. This impact showed me how very deeply I do miss my childhood place, how I somehow belong in a different place than here—as well as here. I've not really questioned where I belong until now. I see that I need an understanding of my "place"—of where I belong, physically as well as emotionally. This I think is very important to everyone. It is certainly very important to me.

At the end of his presentation, Billy presented his three-dimensional graphic, a metaphoric statement of his ideas. He opened a briefcase which he had fitted with mirrors to portray a head radiant with books and ideas, the mirrors extending the image in a series of receding reflections:

This self-portrait represents how my head is filled with the literature that we've read in this class, its ideas reflected in the mirrors of my consciousness. The never-ending series of images shows that the ideas, memories, and feelings that we have all shared as a class this year will keep reflecting, too, and they will affect everything else that any of us read or think.

As this student's words testify, the making of these graphics elicits patterns that have emerged in students' thinking and compels them to evaluate their own place in the scheme of things. We believe very strongly in self-assessment. The graphic dimension provides us with one more way of helping students understand and evaluate their own learning.

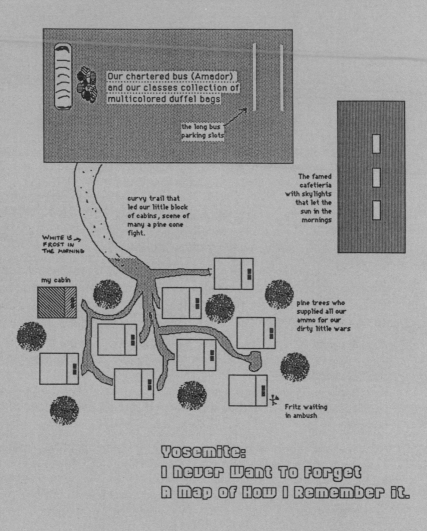

Our chartered bus (Amador) and our classes collection of multicolored duffel bags

the long bus parking slots

The famed cafetieria with skylights that let the sun in the mornings

curvy trail that led our little block of cabins, scene of many a pine cone fight.

WHITE IS FROST IN THE MORNING

my cabin

pine trees who supplied all our ammo for our dirty little wars

Fritz waiting in ambush

Yosemite:
I Never Want To Forget
A Map of How I Remember it.

5-1 Computer Map by Arvind Rao (First Draft)

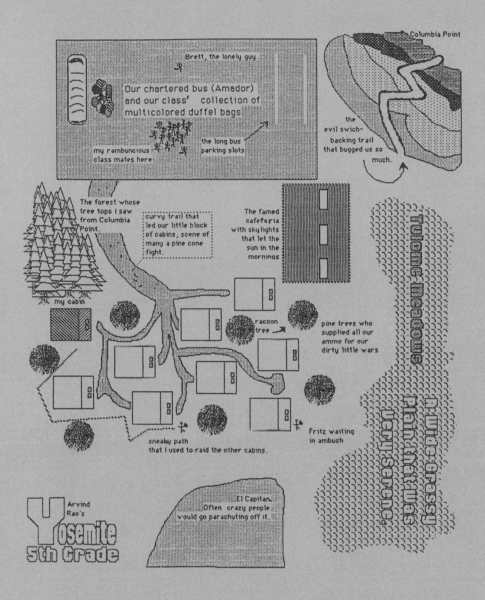

5-2 Computer Map by Arvind Rao (Second Draft)

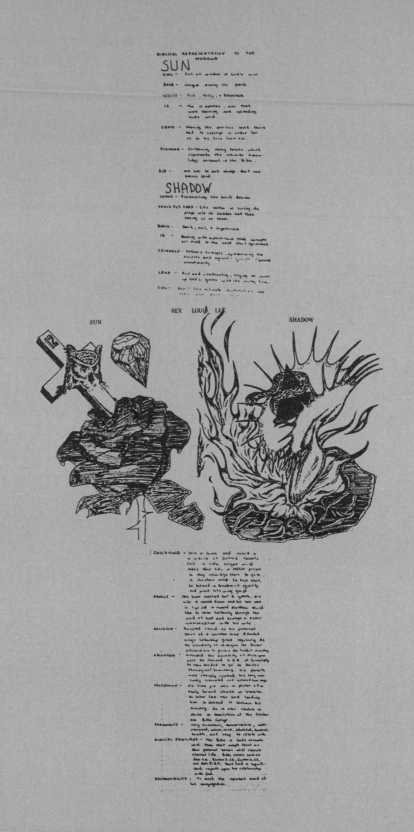

5-3 Interview Map of Reverend Lee by Gary Lym

5-4 "Two Sides to My Father" by Reshma Patel

5-5 "Mandala of Mother" by Julia Ng

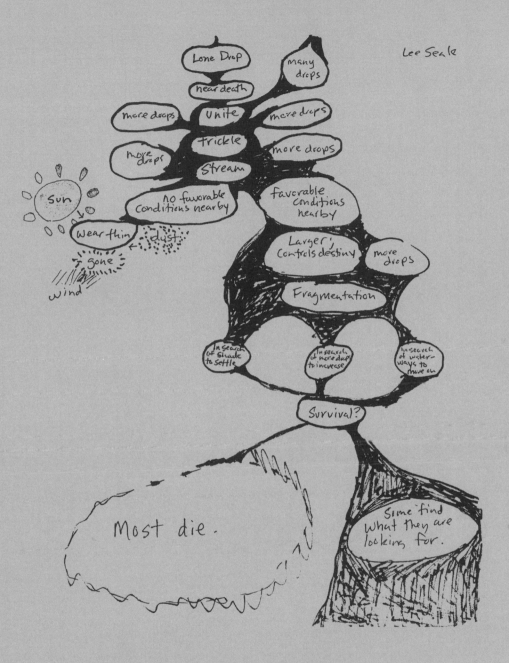

5-6 "A Drop of Water" by Lee Searle

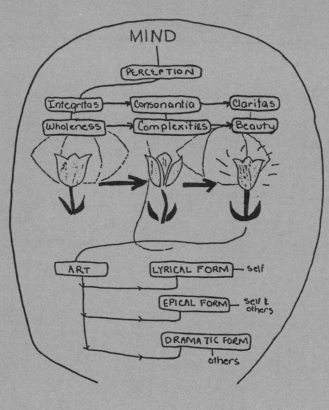

"Integritas, Consonantia, Claritas" by Janet Wong

PART THREE

ANALYSIS AND SYNTHESIS: CHARACTER, STYLE, AND CONCEPT

"Ad pulcritudinem tria requiruntur integritas, consonantia, claritas." I translate it so: "Three things are needed for beauty: wholeness, harmony and radiance." Do these correspond to the phases of apprehension?

STEPHEN DAEDALUS IN JAMES JOYCE'S
A Portrait of the Artist as a Young Man

In Part II, we focused on classroom management: how, when, and why to use the graphic process. Now, in Part III, we turn to the use of graphics to emphasize certain aspects of literary study: character, style, and concept. James Joyce, through Stephen Daedalus, goes beyond Aquinas' theory of the components of beauty to a theory of how we apprehend a work of art. His approach clearly defines the progression of how we use graphics in the full study of literature.

"The first phase of apprehension is a bounding line drawn about the object," said Stephen Daedalus. "You apprehend its wholeness. That is *integritas*." In the classroom, this phase is represented by the graphic and written response log: the student responds first to the work as a whole, recording initial impressions both visually and verbally. "Then," said Stephen, "you pass from point to point, led by its formal lines; you feel the rhythm of its structure. In other words, the synthesis of immediate perception is followed by the analysis of apprehension. That is *consonantia*." When students analyze a work of literature to discover *what* it says and to determine *how* it says it, they have to think critically, to examine closely, to make concrete claims, to draw conclusions, and to organize and state it all with style, with panache.

Such critical thinking and communicating skills are vital for students to develop if they are to succeed in an increasingly complex world—and such skills are not inherent, appearing fully-formed in students once they reach a certain age. The scientist must be trained in the steps of the scientific method, from forming a logical hypothesis to determining how to test the hypothesis, and finally, to drawing conclusions. The student of literature, in a similar yet distinct way, must develop patterns of thinking— to become aware of personal reactions; to develop claims; and to test these claims, looking at how the author uses such elements as character, structure, events, genre choice, point of view.

The graphic activity is one way of providing both the structure and the technique students need to develop analytic thinking. Using literature as their base, students begin by discovering their own responses and formulating a hypothesis. Working alone or in groups, they develop their research skills as they test their hypothesis, molding and re-forming it until it satisfies them; they analyze the work as they integrate text into their graphic and written explorations.

We don't stop with analysis, however. Stephen explained the last step, which corresponds to an essential phase of our process, the presentation of the graphic to the class: "When you have apprehended that basket as one thing and have then analyzed it according to its form and apprehended it as a thing you make the only synthesis which is logically and esthetically permissible," Stephen explained to his friend Lynch. "The instant wherein that supreme quality of beauty, the clear radiance of the esthetic image, is apprehended luminously by the mind which has been arrested by its wholeness and fascinated by its harmony is the luminous silent stasis of esthetic pleasure, a state very like that condition which Luigi Galvani called 'the enchantment of the heart.' "

It is in this phase that the scientific analogy as it is often appropriated by literary critics breaks down; but if the critic were to consider the whole scientific experience as one considers the whole literary experience, it holds: scientist, artist, writer, reader—all begin with a vision, vague and unformed as it may be, the mind "in that mysterious instant Shelley likened beautifully to a fading coal." And all end, after the meticulous experiments, after the analysis of character, of style, of concept, with that re-forming "enchantment of the heart."

The connections begin with looking at the work as a whole, move to the analysis of parts, and become fully synthesized in conveying Galvani's personal enchantments to others who have seen through different eyes, minds, hands.

CHAPTER 6

LITERARY CHARACTER MANDALAS AND GRAPHIC MAPS

But in the peopled world, there is,
Besides the people, his knowledge of them.

WALLACE STEVENS

The peopled world and our knowledge of it extends beyond the narrow range of our immediate community; through literature, film, and television, it knows no boundaries. When we think about novels that have stayed with us long after the reading, we often think first of its peopled world, the characters. If the novel has been a powerful one for us, we have clear pictures of the way the characters look, think, and act. We become possessive of our visual pictures, often protesting when we see a film version of the book that the characters "weren't really like that." Working with both images and words, mandalas and graphic maps help students perceive the complexities of literary characters, understand how they function in drama and fiction, and explore the relationships between them.

Literary mandalas

Because the sun-shadow mandala (see Chapter 2) involves students in working with dualities, it lends itself naturally to an exploration of both external (sun) and internal (shadow) traits of literary characters. While we emphasize the study of literature here, character mandalas are appropriate across the curriculum. History teachers may use the mandala to help students understand the behavior and motivations of historical figures or to look at a person's effect on cultural or world events. Science teachers may use mandalas in graphing the relationship of major scientists and their discoveries or inventions. Whatever the teacher's goals for a specific assignment, the mandala process of interpreting character builds on the larger educational objectives of facilitating the analysis of character motivation and the synthesis of seeing how the many faces a character may wear are all part of a single individual.

SINGLE CHARACTER MANDALAS

Literary sun-shadow mandalas range from quick sketches to highly complex drawings following a comprehensive study of a character in a novel or play. The writing that follows the making of literary mandalas includes identifying sentences, extended metaphors, fully developed poems, and interpretive papers that incorporate metaphoric thinking. The first two examples of literary mandalas, and the poem that accompanies one of them, mark the culmination of a study of *The Great Gatsby*. In Figure 6–1, Mike Molina explores the character of Jordan, building his character study around the playing card the queen of hearts. He places Jordan's shadow-shape, the blue heart for deceit, toward the top of the card; the red heart, sun image for the hidden love that Nick sees inside of her, toward the bottom.

In the second example from *The Great Gatsby*, Geoff Hall examines the character of Owl Eyes. Building his graphic around the joined shapes of the predatory owl (with eye-glasses, reminiscent of the Eyes of Dr. Eckleberg) and its prey, the rat, Geoff uses his sun and shadow images to explore a major issue raised in the text—that of what is real. Both the mandala (Figure 6–2) and the accompanying poem show his clear understanding both of the character of Owl Eyes, and of the importance of this deceptively minor character in the novel.

Geoff's mandala poem:

WHO ASKS

Blind little man from the sea of wheat
    looks across monotony and asks
        Is it real—the lone cactus with diamond spines—

        It must be real.
    Who? The question returns sharply.

Looks with orange radiant whiskers
        Is it real—the brown and average earth—
            it seems real.
    Who? The question runs back slickly.

Looks with glassy rhinestone claws
        Is it real—it looks so clear yet
            he is real.
    Who? The question groans.

Looks through intangible air
        Is it real—the solid ground below me
            It is real.
    Who? The question sighs.

Looks from plotted points
        It is real, repeating
            They are so real.
    Who? The question snaps.

Looks infinitely
            They are so real.
    Who knows.
    He always will.

The mandala process brings students to a deep understanding of character and leads them into sensitive and perceptive writing. The following poem was written by a middle school student after completing a sun-shadow mandala for Buck in *Call of the Wild*.

BUCK

A horse's high-pitched whinny
Echoes in the morning.
The sound,
Like ocean waves
Crashing to the sandy shores,
Brings smiles
To the passers-by
Who roam underneath the
Rising sun.

The comforting aloe vera plant
Intertwined within itself
Thirsts for the cool sea water.
It grows ever so slowly.
Its roots shoot into the ground
As the weeds try to destroy.
Visions of Buck race through
Absent minds.

The horse's whinny fades.
Blue sky turns to clouds
As the sun goes behind
The mountains and disappears.
Night comes once again.
The waves even seem to go to sleep.

Along with the peaceful blowing of
The wind,
A lonely, sleepy bird
Whistles
Its good night tune.

BY CODIE KIDMAN

CHARACTER MANDALAS AND THE RELUCTANT READER

The literary mandala as well as the personal mandala provide an opportunity for students to demonstrate their own ability not only to their classmates but to themselves. A mandala of True Son from *Light in the Forest*, the first piece of work completed by this freshman student, marked a turnaround in his classroom performance that lasted for the rest of the year. This mandala assignment proved to him that he could speak intelligently and perceptively about a character in a work of literature; he could also get well-deserved recognition from other students, a new experience for him. His sun image sentences showed both him and the rest of the class not only that he had read the book, but that he had understood it. Here are some of the sun image sentences that Brad used in preparation for drawing his mandala:

SUN IMAGE SENTENCES

True Son reminds me of an oak tree because he is robust and strong.

True Son is like 11 because, like 11, he is split apart, an Indian who is going to be with the whites.

True Son is like iron, strong, durable and simple.

True Son is like rain because, like rain pouring down, he is crying inside and out to stay with Cuyloga.

True Son is like a straight line because, like this line he has two separated ends: at one end he wants to be with the white family, but at the other end, pulling against it, he wants to be with his Indian family.

EXPLORING CHARACTER THROUGH EXTENDED MANDALA METAPHORS

The extended mandala metaphor technique for building an incremental picture of a single character throughout a book arises from previous student experience with the Sun-Shadow Mandala. Students write extended mandala metaphors appropriate for characters at specific points in the work, explaining their mandala images (animal, plant, shape, etc.) with reasons or references to the text. These metaphoric character images, when clustered on the bulletin board as students proceed through the work, allow students to track character development and change as well as their own growing and changing responses to the character. Their sentences form the basis for continuing class discussion as students compare their choices. Two examples of extended metaphors about characters in *Raisin in the Sun* follow:

In Act 2 of Raisin in the Sun, *Mama is like a fly, frustrated because she is caught in webs of hard times. When she learned that Walter gambled the money away Mama was frustrated both with herself for trusting Walter and with the fact that she couldn't do anything to make him change.*

ALEX CLARK, JUNIOR

In Act 2 of Raisin in the Sun, *Beneatha is like a rock in the ocean because even though she gets slammed a lot, she holds on and never breaks apart in her desire to be a doctor. Even when things look their darkest and it seems like there is never going to be any money, Beneatha still holds on to her dream of becoming a doctor. She just refuses to let anything wear her down or get in the way of her future.*

KRISTIE BROUHARD, JUNIOR

Extended metaphors also provide the basis for full character study mandalas and papers. After students have had time to internalize the process of metaphoric thinking, they write sentences like this one about

Lady Macbeth: "Now she becomes like sandstone, slowly breaking apart." Sandra Hum, writing a paper on the role of the witches in *Macbeth*, begins her paper with this extended metaphor:

The witches of Macbeth *resemble a tesseract in that both are complex and mysterious. A tesseract can be modeled in three dimensions, but this would give a distorted view of the actual figure; a tesseract is four-dimensional. It can be described and explained, but we are incapable of perceiving it in its true light since we can't fully perceive a fourth dimension. The witches are seen as people, yet can disappear, summon spirits, and make accurate prophecies. We cannot explain or understand the powers behind the witches or the powers they possess.*

SANDRA HUM, ON THE WITCHES OF MACBETH

SHOWING CHARACTER CHANGE

The concept of the sun and shadow images reflecting two sides of one character can be modified to show a character at different stages of development or at different points in a work. Students learn to use mandala images progressively as they track a character throughout a work. One teacher gives this assignment to her ninth grade class as they read *My Antonia:*

As you progress through your reading of the book, construct a chart with the names of the characters, a mandala-type symbol for each one, and the reason you selected that symbol. After you have finished the book, if you see that the character has changed, draw a symbol for that character at the end of the book and explain your symbol.

Throughout the study of the novel, students keep their charts, adding secondary symbols as their perceptions of characters grow and change. When the class finishes the book, students draw a completely symbolic graphic showing the relationships among three of the characters. All of the elements of the graphic—shape, color, texture—relate specifically to the student's interpretation of the characters and their interrelationships. Once the projects are completed, each student presents his or her project orally. The members of the group ask questions, offer suggestions, and in other ways contribute to their expanded understanding. Following the oral presentation, each student writes an essay explaining the relationships of the three characters chosen for the project.

The teacher who shared this activity with us wrote, "This activity pulls the students along through the book and appears to enhance the class discussions as students are accumulating proof, if you will, for their feelings and interpretations. What I notice: increased figurative language, deeper interpretations of each of the three characters and their inter-relationships, and more speculation about human nature."

By using the *sun images* to represent a character early in a work and the *shadow images* later, a student demonstrates understanding of character development. In Figure 6–3, Mike Lee uses sun images to show the Juliet seen by her family and friends before she met Romeo: she is a puppet, held immobile in front of a closed door by strings of "shoulds" from her family and her society. The shadow-side of the mandala shows a different Juliet, a more complex woman, as a bird flying free, aiming high, but still caught in a chasm.

Students work either individually or in groups to construct "capture-the-moment" mandalas focusing on characters at particular turning points. This technique works particularly well in the study of a long or complex work. It allows students to explore character motivations in specific instances rather than more generally throughout an entire play or novel; as they finish the work, it allows them to compare the character at the beginning and the end, examining the changes and the catalysts for those changes.

As a freshman class reads *Catcher in the Rye,* students collect sun and shadow images of Holden at different points in the book, keeping records of these ideas in their journals. Periodically, they choose from among these sentences and give them shape to make their extended metaphors into short poems such as these:

Holden is a pyrocantha bush,
       sharp and thorny,
        and
   showing up where he's not wanted.

    Like fool's gold,
Holden appears indifferent,
     but really,
        inside,
    he cares.

Holden is like a scribble,
     all mixed up
       and
     not yet sorted out.

When they finish reading the novel, they work in pairs, choosing from their images to construct mandalas. They then work either in pairs or groups of three or four to write character poems based on their images. One of the group poems uses some of their early fragments to represent Holden:

CHANGES

Stubborn, self-pitying and
    quick to judge,
Holden goes through his life
              alone—
        in his own gray fog.
   Instead

of an arrow
directing
his way, he
w   a   n
d
e
r
s
dreary   and   moping
from the protection of his school
to the
o   p   e   n   and   indifferent streets
of New York.

Like fool's gold,
Holden appears not to care,
but
in the protection of the hospital,
just maybe
he can bloom —— a rose.

The pyrocantha can lose its thorns,
and, as he gains
CONFIDENCE
to rejoin the world,
the fog will burn off
in the sunlight.

BY JENNY BENNHOFF, LEA BRASHEARS,
JEFF BROWN, SARAH ROETHE, AND HOLLY SNOW

Proceeding in such a way—developing a series of mini-mandalas as a work proceeds—encourages students to look closely at character and character motivation as they read, rather than simply to view them in retrospect. Such activities make the classroom a real place of discovery: students, learning together, becoming aware of their own responses as the work proceeds. They are learning to touch, trust, and validate their own responses rather than waiting for the teacher to tell them what to think.

THE RELATIONSHIP MANDALA

Another modification of the sun-shadow mandala shows the relationship between two characters rather than between a character at two points in a story. Students may choose to have one character represent the sun and one the shadow or, not making that distinction, show their overlapping characteristics by having the two mandalas overlap, as in a Venn diagram. In Figure 6–4, Diane Morris explores the relationship between Daisy and Winterbourne in Henry James' *Daisy Miller*, portraying Daisy as the sun-side of the mandala, and Winterbourne as her shadow-side.

HONORS STUDENTS AND METAPHORIC THINKING

Students in honors classes respond to the mandala exercises by trying kinds of writing they often feel they don't have time for in their academic classes. Encouraged to relax—a state of mind that encourages metaphoric thinking—they discover both the freedom and the discipline required by the process of creating. The process of working with mandalas serves as a training ground for incorporating metaphoric thinking into all kinds of writing. We include two brief extracts of interpretive papers here to show the movement from an honors freshman student's very direct use of mandala images to a junior's more sophisticated integration of metaphor into the text of his paper.

In the following passage, an extract from an eight-page character study of Brutus, Michael Chen focuses on the element of *water* as a way of helping to define Brutus' nature. He has dealt with each of the sun-shadow elements as he portrays Brutus in both his actions and his relationships:

Brutus' idealism can best be illustrated by the reference to that powerful, awe-inspiring element of water, for through the honesty of Brutus, his idealism as well as trust caused him to flow as would the liquid in the hands of Cassius, to bend in the grasp of the will of the scheming conspirator. . . . Like water, which could be raised to the climactical extent of torrentous rage, as a river in the midst of thundering downpour, no longer conforming to the mold laid by others, but carving its own path . . . is Brutus also; for when his sheer terror of honesty became dominant with the idealistic visions of perfection, he parallels a crashing flood, in that Cassius could but be swept into consent for his actions. The opportunist in Antony drove him to take as great an advantage of Brutus' other characteristic of water—his ability to conform and flow. Thus Antony molded the situation and Brutus.

Desmond Chin, a junior honors student, had made mandalas at different points in class, though he had not made a mandala as part of his study of *The Great Gatsby*. Still, the influence of training in metaphorical thinking is clear in the thesis paragraph of his final interpretive paper on this novel.

THE WORLD OF PETALS

The world of F. Scott Fitzgerald's The Great Gatsby is a flower consisting of a center and a corolla of petals. The flower itself forms a world which, having survived a war, was now disillusioned and complacent about traditional values and was probing for new codes of morals and understanding. Aspiring flappers and their ardent wooers, many of whom affected an air of bewildered abandonment toward life, came to feed on the nectar which the flower produced. Within this flower was a nucleus, New York, which linked the other three petals together: East Egg, West Egg, and the Valley of Ashes. Together, the nucleus and the corolla formed the East, the world in which Fitzgerald's characters lived; however, each petal and nucleus possessed characteristics of its own kind and was a world separate from the other parts of the flower, influencing and reflecting the actions of the characters.

DESMOND CHIN

The following poem shows the influence of the mandala process as Linda Yee, an Advanced Placement student, integrates both sun and shadow images that reflect her close reading of *Oedipus Rex*.

OEDIPUS IN EXILE

A dolphin's low moan
Echoes in the night.
The sound, like tidal waves
That bash against jagged cliffs,
Irritates the ears
Of suppliants
Who must not hear.

The slick blue fish
Tangles in the meshy trap, is
Plucked from the water.
The grey, still air suffocates.
He twists, wavers back and forth,
Then delivers a
Single acrid cry
Above the tuna's
Floundering splashes.

The brilliant, burning sun
Scorches his eyes.
He can only listen
To the crystal chimes
Of a distant buoy.
They arouse shadows
Of a bright, purple past.

Once, in a dream,
He was a bull,
With horns as swift and sharp
As a diamond's edge.
His head, a flickering ember,
A brute, "whom all. . .call the great,"
Stands as stout as an oak tree
Ready to crush
Commoner or king.
The gates snap open.
He shoots into the ring.
Loud screams muffle his ears.

Run, capture the waving red cloak.
Horns lunge forward
For the kill.

It's gone. He stumbles
And flinches.
A sword grates
Through his eyeballs.

A wave rushes back
Up on shore
and falls
Again and again.
The pain's bitter resonance:
Prickly pine tree thorns
Pinching at the eyes and joints.

LINDA YEE

Literary mandalas, often strikingly original and beautiful, and the writing they engender, provide an easily accessible technique for all students, helping them make connections that make characters real in their lives. For many students, the mandala memory provides a key entry into a life rich with shared literary experience.

Literary maps

Graphic maps, like mandalas, often present a full character study, exploring various aspects of personality and tracking changes. Because the mapping process involves the student in explicit textual validation, students work with more complex elements of character behavior and motivation, still incorporating the metaphoric thinking engendered by the mandala. (See Chapter 2 for basic instructions on how to structure assignments in the graphic map, and Chapter 4 for how to manage them in the classroom.)

The process of making a character graphic is an organizing and integrating activity. It is a way of clarifying ideas and authenticating details visually, an exercise that greatly facilitates verbal expression. Sometimes, through this process, a student discovers the artist within, but an aesthetically pleasing creation is certainly not a condition of success in this activity. Rather, like the mandala, the map is a tool for helping students learn to think, to organize, and to validate their thoughts and ideas.

Although we often construct very specific graphic assignments, we find the responses to be as varied as the students themselves. Participation in the character mapping process, sometimes done in groups, releases students from a fixed perspective and enables them to look at a character from multiple points of view. As students shift between text and drawing—

searching the text for appropriate quotations and appraising the evolving map for placement of word and symbol—they discover that literary characters take on all the dimensions of complex human beings.

PRE-MAPPING: INTRODUCING THE CHARACTER MAP

Just as we use pre-writing, we often use pre-mapping. In another version of the quick-draw that we detailed in Chapter 4, this introductory assignment structures a process for integrating both metaphoric images and using quotations to validate interpretive claims about a character. The instructions are quite specific:

1. List two specific character traits.
2. Draw a symbol to reflect each trait.
3. Write down at least two illustrative quotations linking your impression of the character and the symbol you have chosen.
4. Explain your examples.

Here, David, a freshman, selected the character traits and chose metaphors to represent them. Then he illustrated the metaphors, connecting them with a series of symbols ranging from guns to dogs to hunting hats, all reflecting his perception of Zaroff in "The Most Dangerous Game." The written part of his assignment, which indicates the symbols that he drew, follows the chart:

Character:	*Zaroff from "The Most Dangerous Game"*
Character Trait:	*Hunter and killer*
Symbol:	*The shark*
A quotation:	*God made some men poets. Some he makes kings, some beggars. Me he made a hunter.*
Dave's commentary:	*Just as the shark is born, bred and spends its life hunting and killing, Zaroff knows no other lifestyle. He feels that hunting and killing are his destiny—his purpose in life.*
Character Trait:	*Cunning and crafty*
Symbol:	*The fox*
A quotation:	*One almost did win. I eventually had to use the dogs.*
Dave's commentary:	*Manipulating the situation, Zaroff utilized any available resource to win. He "fixed" all variables, allowing him to play the game of sport without permitting the possibility of failure.*

In this exercise, David shows his engagement in the kinds of thinking—both critical and metaphoric—that lead to strong interpretation. He visualizes his character in terms both of the story and of the world outside of literature. His resulting paper evidenced the original thinking and textual supports that are the hallmark of valid interpretation. It was rich with imagery taken directly from his graphic, and had the strong voice of authenticity and ownership that comes when one knows his subject well.

DEPICTING A SINGLE CHARACTER

Graphics may address the way a character functions within the framework of a whole work. Sometimes we focus on this aspect of mapping to have students create a graphic essay, a visual map for a written character study. As students build a graphic about a character, they illustrate their main idea with textual supports as well as symbols, writing the thesis and supporting quotations directly on the map.

In one such graphic essay, Kim Potter, a junior, shows Nick's place in the world of the East in Fitzgerald's *The Great Gatsby*. Her graphic incorporates and substantiates her thesis statement:

Despite being an active member, Nick was able to recognize the pretentious ways of West Egg society in his heart and mind, and thus rise above as an individual.

The graphic shows an island of society and portrays its inhabitants as circus caricatures trapped in that setting. This visual incorporates and substantiates her thesis statement, which is then validated by the quotations and commentary surrounding the island. The interpretive paper that emerged from this exercise was rich in imagery and in textual support, reflecting Kim's thinking and organizing process in constructing the graphic.

Like Kim, Barry Tribuzio uses a character map to show the relationship of his character—Daisy Miller—to the world in which she lived (see Figure 6–5). Unlike Kim, however, Barry's thesis is not directly stated on his graphic. Rather, he uses the style of the drawing to make his statement about her character. Portraying her as a caricature, bounded by the various elements in her world—the palace, the garden, the Walker party, her new address—he clearly shows his understanding of her place in her world and of the effects of that world on her.

In addition to exploring a character's personality or motivations directly, graphics can address the functioning of a character as symbol. In these graphics, students explore both the personality of the character and the importance of that portrayal to the work as a whole.

Exemplifying the character as symbol graphic, one student, Rodd Schlenker, created a map that explored Dickens' use of Fagin in *Oliver Twist*. His quotations included both physical descriptions of the character and references to his interactions with other characters. Because Rodd's goal was to prove that Dickens uses Fagin as a symbol for the Devil, each quotation he chose specifically reflects Fagin's Satanic quality. Rodd integrated the textual excerpts with his overall symbol of the flames of hell, using reds, oranges, and yellows to reflect the Satanic quality of Fagin.

The conceptual map, which relies exclusively on the selection and placement of symbol, becomes a powerful exercise in visual thinking. These graphics range from very simple depictions which depend heavily on the student's interpretation to convey intent to elaborate drawings that truly convey idea graphically.

Annick Mebine's graphic (Figure 6–6) combines elements of both the mandala and the map to present a simple but perceptive portrait of Delia

Lovell from Edith Wharton's *The Old Maid*. Annick explains her graphic (the reader will have to imagine the colors):

My graphic is like a mandala but not the typical sort. I chose the cat as the animal symbol for Delia—a black/white silhouette because Delia has two faces—one toward society and one in her own world. I wanted to keep the graphic simple, as I usually do, so the person looking at it can see the character directly. For colors, rose was the sun-side; Delia was such a rose. purple and gray were the shadow colors, because Delia was mischievous and dull at the same time. (She was half an Old Maid). The yellow crescent toward the back of the cat represents Delia's adopted daughter, Tina, the light of her life, a constant reminder of Clem (Tina's father, Delia's early love). The snake was Delia's shadow animal—clever and sly. (The snake is also the necklace Delia gave to Tina.) Delia is represented both by number one because she is a straight-laced character; she does what's "right," and by a nine, manipulative and divisible. She is multi-dimensional, following along on the circular treadmill of her life while remaining strongwilled and true to her interior self.

Mimi Nicosia's map of Delia's character is, like Annick's, completely conceptual; rather than using mandala metaphors to generate images, however, Mimi focuses her examination on Delia's two faces through clusters of symbols drawn faithfully from the text. (See Figure 6–7.)

In comparing the two graphics of Delia, we see how differently two students visualize the same character. It is this singularity of voice, which comes through strongly in the mapping process, that we find echoed, often eloquently, in subsequent writing. Following the graphic study of character in *The Old Maid*, for example, students write an original chapter set seven years after the end of Wharton's work. As students speculate about the intervening years, they pick up their own metaphors as well as symbols from the novella and weave them into a compelling narrative extension that Wharton herself might have found provocative.

TRACKING CHARACTER CHANGE

The graphic map enables students to track the changes in a character throughout a work and to explore the effects of those changes, on themselves, on other characters, and on events. One powerful change is the effect of a single emotion on a character's evolution. In Figure 6–8, Joanna Tai explores how fear consumes Ralph in *Lord of the Flies*.

Joanna's understanding of how Ralph was finally consumed by his own inner fear prepared her for writing an assigned monologue in the voice of the character. "I struggled for this image," she said, speaking of her process, "trying to really see what I was trying to say about Ralph and what happened to him and how it would affect him for his whole life. But when I began to write my monologue, it was automatic. Ralph's voice and feelings just flowed out of my pen, and I did it really in a single draft."

The next illustrations in response to a character study of *The Scarlet Letter* show a map (Figure 6–9) along with one view of an accompanying multi-dimensional graphic (Figure 6–10) exploring the role guilt plays in

Dimmesdale's life. Students often choose to work in more than one dimension. They construct elaborate graphics, sometimes with moving parts, often, like the Navaho sand paintings, existing for only one presentation.

This multi-dimensional graphic was accompanied by a clock constructed out of Legos. The students presented the clock to the class, closed and perfect, hands pointing precisely to twelve o'clock. "This," they told the class, "is Dimmesdale as he is perceived by the community— pure, upstanding, and in perfect working order." Then, unlatching a Lego at the top of the clock, they swung open its door to reveal a battery of gears (Figure 6–9) that turned, but only with effort. "This, however," they went on to say, "is Dimmesdale inside, not working nearly so well as it would appear. His gears are somewhat out of joint." Finally, Karen held up a thin black Lego for the class. "This," she told us smugly, "is Chillingworth." She jammed "Chillingworth" into the gears, rendering them completely inoperative. "And this is what he does to the inner workings of our noble minister."

The influence of Karen's work on the graphic becomes explicit in this extract from the thesis paragraph of her paper:

Nathaniel Hawthorne, in The Scarlet Letter, *carefully depicts the silhouette of a man hidden behind a wall of guilt. Arthur Dimmesdale, minister extraordinaire, suffers deeply from his guilt, acknowledged to himself, but hidden away from the rest of his world. In the end, his guilt ravages him from the inside, breaking him down step by step until finally he is destroyed.*

In another example from *The Scarlet Letter*, a student follows a graphic essay assignment to show Pearl's transformation from a subtly evil sprite or elf to a free-spirited woman. The student actually transforms her symbols from a spritelike creature shaped to echo the letter "A," the major symbol in the novel, into a free-spirited bird.

The symbols that students choose to reflect character vary from pictorial images to geometric shapes, often blending one into the other. Sometimes students show change through their use of color, blending colors through the spectrum to reflect the movement of the character, using strongly contrasting colors together to reflect radical changes, while creating subtle blending of color to reflect slower, more subtle change.

In a graphic focusing on the evolution of Telemachus in *The Odyssey*, Rachel Kalish, a sophomore, represents Telemachus as being a ready-to-bloom flower at the beginning of the story, closed up, but with the potential of the fully opened flower at the end. "Telemachus moves from being a little boy, unsure of himself at the beginning and afraid to set out on his quest, to a young man gaining assertiveness," she tells us.

Still, even though he changes, learning to control his impulsiveness and impatience, and taking responsibility for his actions, he is not a full-blown hero at the end. The flower really has to die to complete its cycle and be able to be born again, and although Telemachus has blossomed at the end, he's just not old enough to have gained all the wisdom and experience that the true hero has. All the way through, we see him compared to Odysseus, who, through his obstacles, is learning the same lessons that Telemachus is just beginning to learn—self-control, patience, and assertiveness.

Even when students choose what might be considered an obvious symbol such as the opening of a flower to show the growth of a character, the process of tracking changes involves the student in a constant interaction between drawing and rereading the text for appropriate quotations.

The last graphic in this section depends totally on one metaphor, the single image of the hawk, to integrate the myth of Daedalus and Icarus with the two sides of Stephen Daedalus, Joyce's protagonist in *A Portrait of the Artist as a Young Man*. Viewed one way, (Figure 6–11A) Stephen Daedalus is Icarus who "would fall silently, in an instant." Reverse the graphic, however, (Figure 6–11B), and we have Stephen as Daedalus, "the hawklike man flying sunward above the sea...." (from *Portrait*). He is an artist, with a call to life, "creating proudly out of the freedom and power of his soul, as the great artificer whose name he bore...."

CHARACTER RELATIONSHIPS

Showing the relationships between two characters in a mandala depends completely on a metaphoric approach. In the character map, however, students may show character relationships through a completely verbal, completely conceptual, or integrated approach. These maps, while often quite complex, may be deceptively simple.

The student's graphic in Figure 6–12 demonstrates how a simply constructed map can show a real understanding of character relationships. Vern tracks the change in Ralph and Jack's relationship in *Lord of the Flies* from one of unity and cooperation ("three of us will go on an expedition, me, Jack and Simon"), through the beginning of the split, to the final separation. At the end, Jack is moving toward Beelzebub, "the name of the devil who represents decay, destruction, demoralization, hysteria and panic," while Ralph struggles on toward the mountain, "home of the Greek god of gods, Zeus, symbolizing morality, reasoning, values and all that is good at heart." Vern's clear understanding of the progress of this relationship, and of the way Golding symbolizes it throughout the novel, is evident in the simplicity of his graphic. He uses color, shape, symbol, and words, without fanfare, to state and develop his thesis. Through generating his thesis visually, he found that the interpretive paper organized itself, as he said, "because, I guess I had organized it myself ahead of time."

Students often use images and symbols in idiosyncratic ways. It is only as the student presents the graphic to the class that we can begin to uncover the layer upon layer of thought that has gone into its conception. Linda Nannizi created an almost totally verbal graphic (not pictured) to show the relationship between Charlotte and Delia in Edith Wharton's *The Old Maid*. Visualizing these two characters as linked by time, she uses the ormolu clock, a central symbol from the novella, as her only visual symbol, putting at its base symbols that appear throughout the work to show the interaction and relationship between these two women. Linda has a wealth of textual references, and she uses them consciously to make both an interpretive and an artistic statement. The contrast between the single symbol and the myriad of quotations she incorporates into her graphic make a strong statement of her perception of these characters. Each quotation is placed with purpose around the clock, and through this placement she conveys how the cousins Delia and Charlotte move from similar characteristics, placed near the clock, to differences, placed toward the outer edges of the graphic.

In contrast to such a highly verbal approach, Mimi Nicosia's complex and artistically sophisticated conceptual graphic explores the relationship of Frank, the major character in John Galsworthy's *The Apple Tree*, to each of the two women whom he has loved. (See the frontispiece to the introduction of the book for this graphic.) Framing the graphic are words from Keats' "Ode on a Grecian Urn," which contains the philosophy that is at the heart of Frank's dilemma in the novella. The poetic frame not only calls it to mind but also demonstrates graphically the structure of the novella: Frank and Stella, celebrating their twenty-fifth anniversary, frame the extended flashback which depicts his early, unconsummated love for Megan, the natural, unspoiled child of nature. Megan, the Aphrodite figure, is depicted as fragile and defenseless, like the apple blossoms in full bloom; while Stella, cultivated and cultured, is Diana, cool and calm, virginal and sensible. Frank, torn between the two, in the end is Hippolytus, choosing one goddess, rejecting Aphrodite. Yet, as in the play *Hippolytus*, which Frank is reading in the novella, Aphrodite gets her final revenge. Although this graphic does explore the relationship of Frank to both Megan and Stella, it also maps the structure of the novella and shows its philosophical parallel with the ode.

6-1 "Jordan" by Mike Molina

6-2 "Owl Eyes" by Geoff Hall

6-3 "Juliet" by Mike Lee

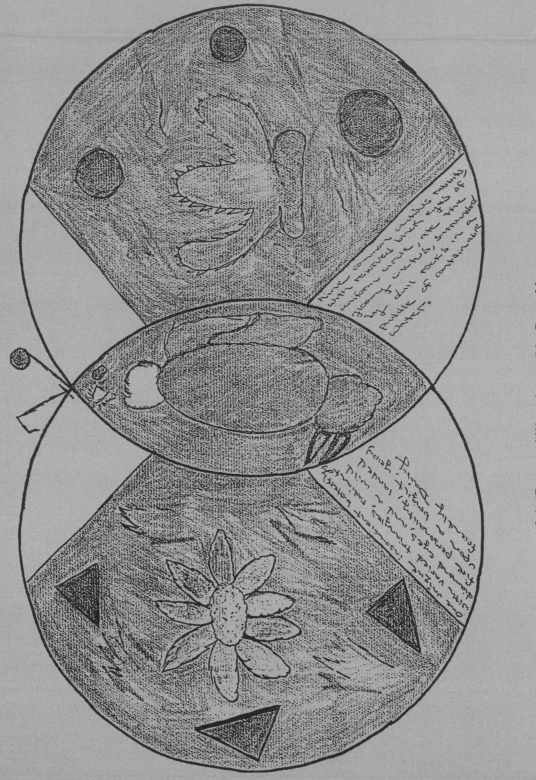

6-4 "Daisy and Winterbourne" by Diane Morris

6-5 "Daisy Miller" by Barry Tribuzio

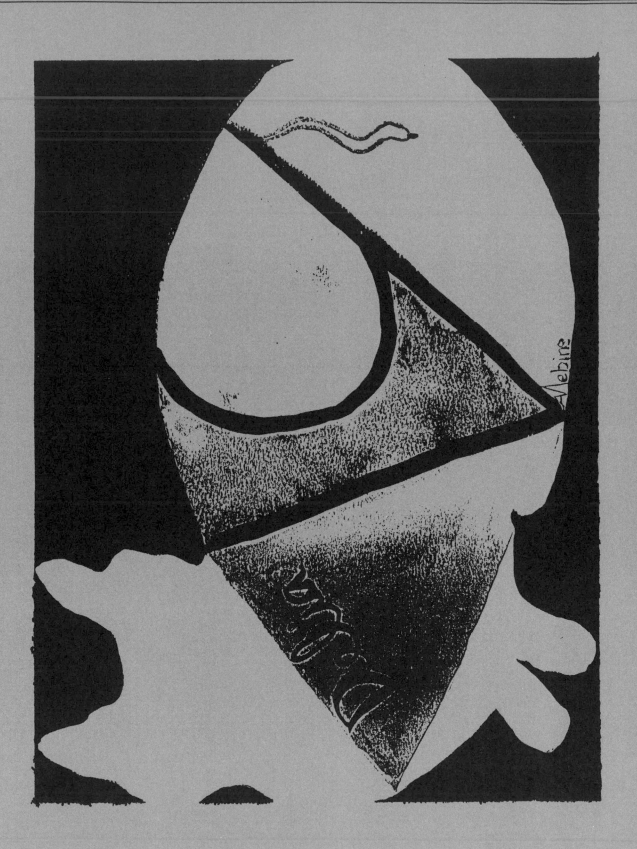

6-6 "Delia" by Annick Mebine

6-7 "Delia" by Mimi Nicosia

6-8 "Ralph" by Joanna Tai

6-9 Inner Works of Dimmesdale-graphic by Karen Gee
and Catherine Dicksen

6-10   Inner Works of Dimmesdale-clock
by Karen Gee and Catherine Dicksen

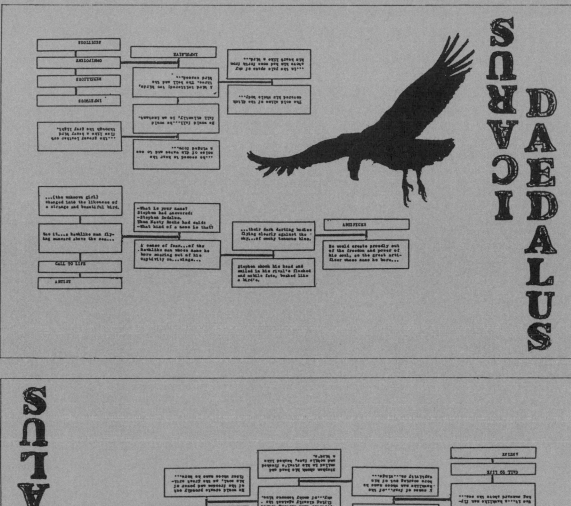

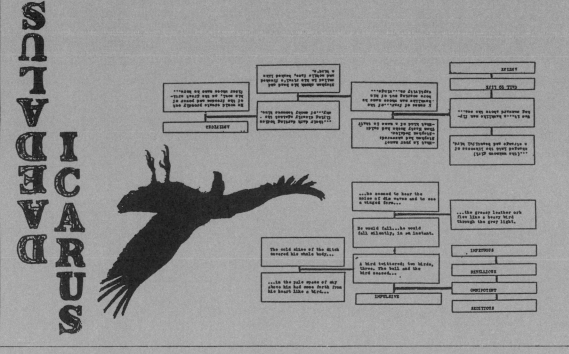

6-11A "Daedulus" by Richard Wong

6-11B "Icarus" by Richard Wong

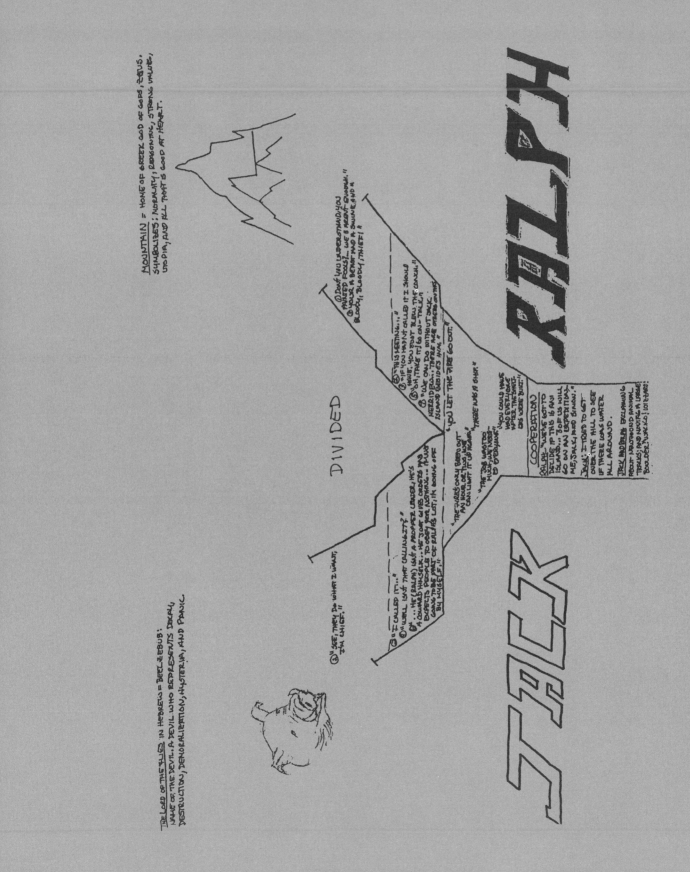

6-12 "Ralph and Jack" by Vern Keller

CHAPTER 7

**MAKING
CONNECTIONS**

When we try to pick out anything by itself,
we find it hitched to everything else
in the universe.

JOHN MUIR

The study of literature is incremental. As the year progresses, we move
through discussions of poems, novels, plays, and non-fiction. Ideas and
motifs recur, cast in words defined by time period or genre, gender,
cultural background, individual bent of mind. Periodically we stop in our
study of individual works to look back on these ideas, to explore how the
same sky appears to different eyes; how the themes of war and love and
freedom unfold in different words when experienced by different minds. In
short, we make connections.

Mandalas, by their very nature, ask students to connect. The circle itself
is contained, bringing students to a visual realization that literature, like our
lives, deals with basic ideas that are framed within the compass of
common experience. In constructing thematically based maps, students
link not only individual works, but historical, social, economic, political,
and psychological elements. Like a road-map, the thematic graphic not
only helps students understand where they've been; it also brings them at
least a glimpse of where they're going.

The movement from the study of individual works to the process of
making connections is a gradual one beginning with the reflective quick-
draws, quick-maps, and written logs described in Chapter 4. As graphics
of different works begin to cover the walls of the classroom, students
naturally integrate and connect and build, exploring recurrences and
variations within discourse types, among different works by the same
author, in recurrent motifs and archetypal themes. At some points, we
make our study of these connections specific and ask students to look
back consciously at other things they have studied—in our class, in
previous English classes, and in classes of other disciplines. From their
multiple impressions and memories, they select themes that mean
something to them; they then begin to construct their own thematic
graphics. The movement mirrors that of Stephen Daedalus' ideas about
the apprehension of beauty in Joyce's *Portrait of the Artist*, which itself
echoes the larger context of learning: we begin with a personal response
to the whole, move to an analysis of its parts, and finally experience
claritas, perceiving the whole with a new understanding. The process is
recursive under any of the possible umbrellas—discourse type, author,
motif, or archetypal theme.

"Author! Author!" A style study

In speaking and writing, as in daily life, we develop certain habits of combining materials, so that we do not have to think through each combination each time. Our habits make our style.

JOSEPHINE MILES

Style is how we recognize a writer, yet when it comes to definition, we're hard put to explain it. "Thought and meaning are inseparable from each other," Cardinal Newman wrote. "Style is a thinking out into language." This statement, like so many others which attempt to deal with style, seems lucid when read, but begins to muddy in retrospect. I. A. Richards suggests in *Practical Criticism* that "many of the secrets of 'style' could ... be shown to be matters of tone, of the perfect recognition of the writer's relation to the reader in view of what is being said and their joint feelings about it." It is these "joint feelings" teachers have begun to elicit and honor as the profession moves toward realizing the ideas of Richards, Rosenblatt, and other theoreticians and critics. It is these "joint feelings" that we hope students come to in their graphic explorations of authors' styles.

The study of style, like the study of myth, in the essential sense, is one of the constants in any English curriculum. Culturally, we learn through *mimesis*, a basic urge to imitate at an archetypal level. There are times, however, when we want to take a conscious look at this thing called style, both to account for the joint feelings we experience when we read and to extend our understanding of how we express our own "habits," as Josephine Miles uses the word.

In preparing students to select one author for an intensive style study, we have them look first at the stylistic elements of three writers they have read and liked. To solidify their impressions and analyses, students construct a graphic map comparing such stylistic elements as subject matter; use of locale; sentence structure and diction; and recurring themes, symbols, or ideas. Students begin their comparison maps by selecting one dominant symbol for each of the authors. Once students have completed their comparisons, they select one of the three authors for an intensive study. We urge them to work in pairs or small groups to encourage collaboration during the study and presentation of their author to the rest of the class.

We assign the reading for the single-author style studies about a month before we begin the class activities, providing perhaps one period a week for in-class reading. During that time, students read at least three novels or a major selection from a body of poetry. Students keep careful, dated log entries of their responses as they read, using quick-draws or sketches as well as personal response and interpretive commentary. These logs form a visible record of their thinking and provide the groundwork for student self-evaluations as well as for our assessment of their work. The activities that evolve from this study usually take another two weeks. They include a comprehensive graphic of the author, focusing on stylistic elements, a short emulation of a typical passage, a substantial story or poem in the style of the author, an interpretive study of some aspect of the author's work, and a presentation to the class.

The emulation, a word-for-word model of a passage or poem that they feel exemplifies their author's style, helps them internalize stylistic features. Cardinal O'Neill, in his study of Wallace Stevens, chose to emulate "Thirteen Ways of Looking at a Blackbird." Before he wrote his emulation, he constructed a graphic, isolating and highlighting his own thirteen ways of looking at a turtle. He translated each stanza of the poem into one picture of his map, which became the basis for his emulation. His final graphic contained the thirteen drawings and the emulation, which follows:

THIRTEEN WAYS OF LOOKING AT A TURTLE

  (after Wallace Stevens)

I.   *Where a frisbee had fallen*
    A turtle now walks
    With life.

II. *Through the sad eyes of a man*
    You see sadness.
    Through the sad eyes of a turtle
    You see knowledge.

III. *A dog*
    Is man's best friend.
    A Man
    Is Turtle's Worst Enemy

IV. *Plowing through the destruction,*
    A tank
    A Weapon of War.
    Walking through life,
    A turtle,
    Messenger of Peace.

V.   *On land*
    It is patient.
    In water
    It is free.

VI. *Through life*
    Things give birth and die
    Everyday
    The turtle
    Stands immortal.

VII. *A mobile home*
    Parks for the night.
    A turtle
    Stops and sleeps.

VIII. *Home is a man's castle.*
    The turtle
    Is the emerald knight
    Of his castle.

IX. *We rush*
    To do all the things
    In such short time.
    A turtle
    Has patience.
    He will live forever.
X. *A turtle is harmless in the eyes of man.*
    In his world
    It may be considered a giant.
XI. *Some old men want to die.*
    Some old men fear flying.
    The turtle has no fear of death.
XII. *Through life*
    Man gained knowledge.
    The turtle is knowledge.
XIII. *The grass*
    Green as it is,
    Winds whispering blissfully.
    All life is focused on the turtle.

CARDINAL O'NEILL

Figures 7–1 and 7–2 show very basic single author maps. In Figure 7–1, a verbal graphic of Robinson Jeffers, Lori Cheung organizes her material visually to show the major emphases in her study: life and times, critical conclusions, and style of writing, which includes Jeffers' use of motifs and symbols.

Three students collaborated to graph their study of Faulkner after reading and discussing *The Bear*, "Race at Morning," "Barnburning," and Faulkner's Nobel Prize speech. This graphic, shown in Figure 7–2, depends on the portrait of Faulkner to hold it together; the symbols that appear on the map are placed near appropriate information. These students used the mapping process to record substantial sections of information, which they made use of in their group presentation and, individually, in their "stories in the style of" or interpretive papers.

In contrast to these highly verbal maps, Figure 7–3 displays what a more visually oriented student has chosen to do with this graphic assignment. Mimi Nicosia's selection of Kenneth Patchen points to her interest in a visual poet: Patchen's poems are nearly all embedded in his own artwork. In her graphic, Mimi echoes Patchen's visual style by creating a pastiche of Patchen's own books, symbols, and words to convey her sense of him as an artist.

As students construct these graphics, using all four functions—observe, analyze, imagine, feel—they become conscious of how a writer uses the elements of style to create subtleties of meaning. Because students are engaged in exploring their joint feelings about "the writer's relation to the reader" and "their joint feelings about it," they become involved with the author on a very personal level. Their understanding comes from their own discernment, rather than simply appearing as lecture notes on binder paper in a notebook, augmented by a variety of secondary sources.

Although students often work collaboratively on their graphics, they are each responsible for writing an individual analytical paper on some aspect of the author's style. Their graphics group, however, provides a natural writing response group to help them test out ideas, revise, and edit. The thesis paragraph of Gretchen Anderson's stylistic analysis of *The Bear* shows the influence of the metaphoric thinking that went into her graphic (see Figure 7–3) and emerged from her work with her writing group.

The winding, twisting thrill of a roller coaster, rushing at 90 miles per hour, never slowing, despite quick sharp drops, leaves the rider energized long after the ride is over. This is the effect William Faulkner has on his audience in "The Bear." As Ike forages through Faulkner's jungle of words, he learns a set of values which are to last him the rest of his life. In keeping with Faulkner's idea that "man will prevail," the idea that dominates his Nobel Prize Acceptance Speech, Ike also manages to survive in the face of drastic changes by retaining those values so dearly learned by him. Powerfully packed with insight, Faulkner's words echo the meaning, leaving behind distinct impressions which will remain long after the pages have yellowed with age.

The culminating activity for the style study is the presentation of authors to the class. Presentations must be more than lecture. Student ingenuity has resulted in videotapes, dramatizations, and mock author interviews as well as graphically presented panels and discussions. The oral presentations, which at first seemed only an adjunct to the entire assignment, have emerged as powerful parts of the process of making meaning collaboratively. It is in these presentations that we are often able to perceive the effects of the graphic process on thinking. Students, in talking about their graphics, frequently have sudden, illuminating insights. The graphic recurrently provides the touchstone for comprehension; the process of graphing often precedes conscious understanding of the interrelationships and significance of the elements of the maps.

Here are some extracts from the transcript of the oral presentation made by the Faulkner study group:

Faulkner's themes represent all walks of life. A snake shedding its skin is like life changes: you do away with something, yet you still remain the same through and through, at the depths of yourself. Boon's inability to accept change—to shed his skin, yet hold on to his truths—was tragic; but Faulkner's inherent belief in man's strength is seen in Ike who walks off into the glorious light of the sun, able to face the odds that he knows what lies ahead, and having the courage to set out into a changing world.

As we submerged ourselves within Faulkner's words, we began to understand the style and depth he has—to understand why he insists on writing page long sentences punctuated by semi-colons and parentheses. His sentences go on and on parallelling his belief that man too will go on and on, even though he may not always be absolutely sure of his direction. This optimistic feeling that is in everything we read by Faulkner made us optimistic too: we can go on without compromising our own "old verities and truths of the heart" while embarking on the changing era that lies before us today.

The style study of a single author has ramifications for the development of a student's own style. As students emulate a passage; write a piece in the style of the author; graph the elements of style; talk, argue, and compromise with their groups; and present their understanding to the class, they come to fundamental insights into their own styles.

"Is it useful to be aware of one's own style," Josephine Miles asked in her exploration of what style is all about; "or does such awareness interfere with being natural? My belief is that, once having become conscious of the possible choices and once having made the choices, one can be secure in them and they can become natural. Knowledge and conscious choice, in other words, support rather than oppose intuition, and give it flexibility as well as ease, sympathy as well as surety, a sense of alternatives as well as a sense of preferences." From these words, we take our cue. We urge our students to put on other writers' styles just to get the feel of them, of their habits. When they find a writer whose style feels familiar, when they say, "It's almost as if I had written that!" we encourage them to play with a short emulation. They choose their own subject, but follow the thinking process and grammatical patterns of the author; and when they reach the end of the passage they are modeling, they continue to write, capturing the cadences of the other writer in their own. They develop habits.

Exploring motif

Motif: A recurrent word, phrase, situation, object, or idea. Any repetition that helps unify a work by recalling its earlier occurrence and all that surrounded it.

A Dictionary of Literary,
Dramatic, and Cinematic Terms
BARNET, BERMAN, BURTO

Using graphics to explore motifs in literature provides a continually changing scenario for the classroom. In the process of designing a graphic to show how a motif works in a novel, for instance, groups explore plot, structure, and language; they end up being able to articulate their understanding of many of the elements that contribute to the power of the work.

Although we will be using examples from literature, the tracing of a motif is certainly appropriate in history, science, and art. For example, the theme of the immigrant experience in American history not only stretches back into our past, but reaches into every aspect of our contemporary life. In a study of the immigrant experience, students take advantage of experiences of their own families, themselves, and their classmates as they trace this dominant motif in American culture. (See Chapter 4 for illustrations of student work on this subject.) The graphic portrayal of how a motif changes or echoes throughout a work can make a point more memorably than either talk or text alone. Working usually in groups, students discover and graph the fugue-like appearances and transformations, recurrences and convergences, similarities and variations of motifs.

To see some of the patterns of how we use graphics to explore motifs, we have divided this section into a look at graphics that focus on exploring a single motif, the transformation of a motif, contrasting or parallel motifs, and multiple motifs.

A SINGLE MOTIF

When a symbol or theme emerges as a dominant force in a work, it naturally becomes the primary focus for organizing ideas about the elements of a work. In Galsworthy's novella *The Apple Tree*, for example, the title itself announces the motif that comes to embody all of the dualities that emerge in the development of the story. In Figure 7–4, you can see how Michelle Mebine uses this primary motif of the apple tree as the controlling symbol for her graphic.

The evolving process of conceiving and constructing this deceptively simple map allows Michelle to crystalize her understanding of this work. Her graphic focus on the dominant symbol of the apple tree lets her play with this symbol visually and come to a greater internal understanding of how Galsworthy uses it structurally—to link the present and past, and to signify the deciduous nature of character relationships. Not only did Michelle come to understand this particular story in more depth, she also began to develop an understanding of how writers use symbol.

In contrast to Michelle's ability to work directly with abstraction, a group of freshmen came to understand motif through what began as playful visual punning. In their presentation to the class, they unveiled their graphic study of Romeo and Juliet, a collage of magazine cut-outs of Hollywood star-crossed lovers—Taylor-Burton, Mickey-Minnie, etc. Although a clever pun on Hollywood stars and the star-crossed Romeo and Juliet, this display didn't have the textual validation that we require in this particular graphic study. To our relief, however, the students went on to detail the motif of star-crossed lovers in a second map containing both quotations and commentary.

The graphic assignment allowed these freshmen to take Shakespeare home with them, to play cut-outs, include him at their dinner tables. Once they were relaxed with Shakespeare, the play, its themes and characters, and with the relationship between these ideas and those we had discussed in class earlier in the year, the analysis came easily. Working with images softened the difficulty of analyzing Shakespeare and helped them see connections. "It was a hard thinking project, but we had lots of fun doing it," one student said; "and the thinking part got easier as we went along."

Color as motif can provide the focus for a graphic study. In a starkly red and white visual, Dawn Major traced Hardy's use of these colors in *Tess of the D'Urbervilles*. The quotations on her graphic show the recurrence of and interplay between passion and purity throughout the novel; but they don't show how Dawn's combing of the text looking for *red* and *white* led her to become more and more conscious of Hardy's intention. She came to see that Hardy's use of the color reflected in the concrete images of *fire*, *flushed faces*, *teeth*, and *sea pearls* was at some level deliberate.

In another exploration of duality and color, Carol Dwyer began the thesis for her interpretive paper as a direct outgrowth of her graphic exploration: "Using light and dark imagery, Charles Dickens creates two opposing worlds in his novel *Oliver Twist* to show the dramatic division of classes in Victorian society." In her black and white graphic, Carol documented the light and dark motif through quotations and drawings that contrasted day and night, heaven and hell, the devil and the angel. Students' observation and analysis of an author's use of color as motif, as in these examples, is directly related to their own understanding of how they use color symbolically in their own graphics and writing.

THE TRANSFORMATION OF AN IDEA

Understanding how the basic motif of a work becomes transformed, often into its opposite, becomes accessible for students as they portray the change graphically. Once having visualized the transformation of an idea—how it develops and why—and having linked this change to the events that triggered it, students are able to articulate how an idea or symbol evolves.

Judi Rich used color as well as shape and spacing to illustrate her graphic perception of the transformation of fear into evil in *Lord of the Flies*. Moving from soft yellows and blues in the word "fear" into the red-black end of the spectrum as the "evil" grows out of the fear, she shows the transformation that occurred on the island as the boys' fear gradually overcame them, reducing them to a state of savagery and evil.

Below is part of the thesis paragraph of a paper that emerged from Alice Chuck's study of the motif graphically portrayed by Judi Rich.

"Fear is the mind killer. Fear is the little death that obliterates all others." This statement, from Frank Herbert's Dune, *is equally applicable to Golding's* Lord of the Flies, *a novel written twenty-five years earlier. This work, the story of children isolated on an island during a war, shows vividly Golding's belief in the dominance of the "dark" side of human nature. . . . In civilization, the fear was suppressed by the laws and conformity of society; but as this order breaks up, fear grows. Instinct takes over reason. Conscience, morals and rules have no place in instinct. And so this fear becomes the "little death" that, in the end, "obliterates all others.*

ALICE CHUCK

A graphic on the same theme illustrates what can be done by students who think that they just can't draw no matter how hard they try (Figure 7–5). Moving from four perfectly formed, separate shapes, Sandy Brophy showed the growing chaos on the island in *Lord of the Flies* by varying and combining her shapes and colors. Although Sandy began by thinking that she couldn't draw, her success in communicating an idea graphically led to a new sense of her capabilities. For her, this exercise was one of self-discovery and re-definition as well as an exploration of literature.

CONTRASTING OR PARALLEL MOTIFS

In addition to envisioning the transformation of an idea, students also use graphics to examine contrasting or parallel motifs. The umbrella theme of dualities pervades much of the literature we read and leads to provocative sun-shadow mandala imagery within the broader framework of the graphic map. An example of a graphic presenting the theme of dualities is Mike Egan and Doug Alexander's exploration of reality and illusion in *Hamlet* shown in Figure 7–6. Within the physical setting of a map of Denmark, one reality in the play, they place the overlapping characters that surround Hamlet. They show that there are those who know and those who don't know; there are those who obscure reality on purpose, and those who fail to see truth. The meaning that they come to through their group efforts is that reality and illusion are constantly shifting in this play, as both concepts are dependent on perception.

Another example of the reality/illusion duality is slightly modified into the dream/reality motif in Steinbeck's *Of Mice and Men*. On a background of symbols found in the novel (the farm, the barn, the rabbits, the gun) two sophomores explored the difference between George and Lennie's dream and the reality in which they live. A stark line marks the difference between the dream and their reality—a line that in the end could only be erased by Lennie's death, symbolized on the graphic by a gun. Both the symbols and the quotations on this graphic are placed conceptually rather than chronologically, showing the students' understanding of the relationship between the action in the text and the symbols and ideas reflected by this action.

MULTIPLE MOTIFS

Although we often have students pursuing such specific assignments as these explorations of single or contrasting motifs, we trust the sharing process of the presentations to prevent the tunnel vision that would constrict a student's view of a work to a single aspect. We do, however, also have students look at how multiple motifs can be interwoven in the same work. Here the focus also leans toward the structure of the novel as students see how the development of each motif influences the development of the others.

One example of using graphics to explore multiple motifs in a work is a project that we have seen work with a number of novels and plays in many different teachers' classrooms. This highly structured assignment works well with students of all ages and ability levels. Middle school and junior high school students, for example, work more efficiently when given specific steps to follow; older students work collaboratively with very little direction, once they understand the concepts.

One teacher describes the assignment:

My freshman college prep class had read through Huck Finn, *keeping a reading log with quick-draws and personal responses. Through general discussion, the class chose a central symbol which would unify all of their group graphics; they chose, not surprisingly, the river.*

Students isolated several motifs that seemed to recur throughout the book, drawing from their reading logs; as a class, they chose a symbol for each motif. Freedom, for example, was symbolized by broken chains; Huck's growth, a burning letter; friendship, a handshake. We then rolled out five long strips of butcher paper and drew a river across them all. With each of five groups accepting responsibility for one-fifth of the book, students plotted the action of the novel, placing different events along the river. They added quotations, commentary, and symbols to indicate the meaning of each event within the framework of the novel.

The process for this activity:

First, each student skimmed the assigned section and wrote down five pivotal events. Then, in groups, they chose from their combined lists which events to include on their section of the graphic. Students had four days of class time to work on their sections, and they worked at home as well. Individual group members accepted responsibility for keying events to the motifs and for writing commentary on the graphic during the class period.

The final graphic, then, presented the entire book stretched out along the river, providing the basis for our discussion of the novel as a whole. The ideas we were tracking were all there, and the students could see how each section raised and developed issues of both character and theme progressively through the book.

This study process led students into their final papers in which each student discussed one element of the work, tracking it throughout. Students made widespread use of the graphic wall as they worked on their papers. (See Figure 7–7 for an example.)

The thematic unit

Thematic units generally evolve over a substantial block of time in which students read and study a number of works from a variety of genres. Often students draw on a wide range of sources ranging from literary works to informational documents, from interviews to personal experiences. Although in this section we focus on graphics that mark the culmination of thematic units, we incorporate the full range of metaphoric study and graphic processes that we have described throughout this book.

The graphic record students compile during the year provides a visual as well as a verbal record of their developing understandings; as patterns emerge, they have a palpable base of experience on which to draw. Because class discussions are recursive, students find that they regularly look back at what they have done, re-forming their ideas to fit new configurations. In this sense, then, we are never really finished with a work or a unit. Often our study of literature will emerge as clusters, beginning with the deep study of a central work, and including, as we proceed through our study of that work, poems, essays, and other shorter works that echo the primary motifs.

One archetypal theme that effectively provides cohesion for a unit of many different kinds of literature is the heroic quest. An example of such a project is encapsulated in an incremental graphic, which, while not illustrated here, depicted Billy Tsai's attempt to portray his growing understanding of man's search for peace and understanding. The unfolding nature of the graphic itself replicated the stages of the quest.

The cover depicted the ultimate goal, "Man's Search for Peace and Balance" by using the archetypal dove of peace interwoven with the words of the title. In his presentation, Billy raised this cover gradually, revealing a seated figure covered with quotations from works that Billy had read throughout the semester. The quotations, drawn from a rich variety of historical eras and cultural roots, reflected various stages in the human quest. It is not until the figure was fully revealed that we were able to see the final goal, represented as a serene statue of Buddha, which, he told us,

symbolizes the essence of peace and harmony that all people search for through their lives. The person in this position, like Buddha, has seen the whole picture. He has put all the pieces together and everything seems, finally, so clear. Indeed, at this point, the search is over . . . and ready to begin again.

As students work graphically to integrate their ideas about an entire unit, they have an opportunity to reflect—to put into perspective the things that we've done in our class, and to relate them to their lives. The graphic process, with its dimensions of personal reflection, group brainstorming, kinesthetic visualization, and full-class sharing, is one way in which we can help students continually reframe their lives in terms of new experiences.

In the senior year, in some classes, we begin with a review of basic mythic thought patterns—the heroic quest, the fall from innocence, dualities, and cycles of nature. (See Peter Stillman's book *Introduction to Myth*, Boynton/Cook, 1985.) Each student selects one of the mythic themes to track during the entire semester or year. As the semester progresses, they discover manifestations of their selected myth as they see it in literature, art, advertising, news stories, and their own experiences. At the end of the year, students graph their myth; as part of their final project, they write an original poem, essay, or story tying their myth in some way to contemporary life. Figure 7–8, "Dualities, A Graphic Essay" by Richard Paul, illustrates the graphic element in the assignment, while the following poem, "Prometheus Has Escaped," represents the written element for Barry Tribuzio. Barry is one of many students who discovered in this class his power as both a visual and a verbal artist. (See the Endpiece to "Balancing the Curriculum: An Afterword" for one of Barry's graphics.)

PROMETHEUS HAS ESCAPED

Prometheus has escaped
from the sunsplashed stone
where the eagle dives
only to come up
with tarnished chain.

He has escaped,
to release the fire
with the flick of a switch.
He blinks.
His cufflinks hide
the screaming scars of his past.
A tailored suit assails him now
behind a desk of marble,
a civilized sculptured altar
of corporate sacrifice.

But he has made the true
escape from reality's pain
to consolidated gain,
his name etched in brass
and his life in code
on a chip stored away.
He is no more loved here
than caressed by the talons
and cold hard rock.

Eaten up inside by
the schedules of life,
broken by the whip
of market trends,
'Time is Money'
and the clocks on the wall.

But these things do not occur to him.
He sullenly scratches
the healing itch of his belly
and calls for coffee.
Ankles bound in shined shoes,
he reclines,
lost in the grasp
of padded vinyl,
and the pigeons gather
outside for a feast.

BARRY TRIBUZIO

The graphic map and mandala shown in Figure 7–9 and the accompanying student presentations illustrate the layers of insight and integration that can arise from a thematic unit. This unit moved from a close study of the Antigone theme, as depicted by both Sophocles and Anouilh, to an exploration of the more global theme of civil disobedience expressed in personal interviews, music, and art as well as in literature. The mandala integrates the elements of the study in a global way, while the map organizes the elements metaphorically. The graphics and discussions led to personal position papers in which students identified and clarified their own values.

In this thematic sun-shadow mandala, Sarah and Sharon explore the issue of civil disobedience itself. Through their sun and shadow sentences, they examine this multi-dimensional issue, drawing on specific examples from literature and history. The examples are wide-ranging, from the Boston Tea Party and the American Revolution to the student sit-ins of the sixties, to Antigone, Miss Jane Pittman, and contemporary rock groups.

Examples of extended metaphors that appear on the mandala show the breadth of understanding that developed as these students integrated ideas from widely disparate sources:

"Civil disobedience is a cattle prod that evokes a reaction through shock" refers to the Boston Tea Party and the American Revolution as movements that prodded a reaction.

"Civil disobedience is a daisy, with roots that go deep and are indestructible" and *"Civil disobedience is crabgrass, rooted everywhere, waiting for a little nurturing to grow"* refer to The Autobiography of Miss Jane Pittman.

"Civil disobedience is a screwdriver that works subtly and manually" refers to the works of Martin Luther King and Ghandi.

"Civil disobedience is a flock of mallards whose power lies in their numbers" refers to student sit-ins through the 60's and the Free Speech Movement that began in 1964.

"Civil disobedience is not field mice who run and hide" refers to Ismene's line in Sophocles' Antigone: *"We must remember that we two are women so not to fight with men."*

"Civil disobedience is a pearl growing in reaction to an irritant" is in response to *"Civil disobedience is the result of extreme frustration felt by those who could not get answers through legal methods,"* a direct quotation from an interview with one of the student's grandmothers.

Doug Alexander and David Paiva, who explored the issue of civil disobedience using a map rather than the mandala, chose the image of a tree as their unifying metaphor. (See the Frontispiece to the book for the Civil Disobedience Tree graphic.) Their presentation, excerpts of which we transcribe here, shows the roots and branches of their understanding— their growing awareness of the complexity of change, and of the personal risks that it can entail.

TRANSCRIPT OF STUDENT PRESENTATION OF CIVIL DISOBEDIENCE TREE

The tree represents authority, and all trees go through a number of changes, just as authority and government do. Civil disobedience can affect some, while leaving the rest unchanged. This is why there are so many branches on our tree left unchanged.

The lightning destroying the tree represents revolution, or a physical change in government or authority that might bring it down. The rain falling on the tree's leaves and branches represents the slower change or growth of government or authority in a peaceful manner. We've put both green and brown leaves on our tree of authority. The large mass of green leaves looming over the smaller mass of dying brown leaves represents the idea of the majority overpowering the minority. The majority leaves sometimes block the growth of the minority leaves, and, though the majority is not always right, it is generally the most powerful.

The growing green branch represents the new ideology as illustrated by both Ghandi and Martin Luther King. Each opened a new door by fighting racism and prejudice and, through consistent persistence, making millions think. Both by example and through what they said, these two men opened up new branches of thinking to masses of people, enabling change, however slowly, to begin to be realized.

At the top of our tree stands a single leaf, representing the individual standing alone, separate from the others. This respect of the individual, which we saw in Antigone with Creon's refusal even to listen to Antigone's argument, and which we continue to see today, is vital if people are to retain authority over themselves.

When we went into this project, it was just an assignment we had to get done by Tuesday, but when we really got into it and started to talk about it with our families, we became really involved. When you asked at the start of our reading of Antigone if there was any issue we'd take a risk for, we really couldn't think of one—not that we would, for instance, risk college for. But now that we've thought about it, we do think its important to find the courage to stand up for ourselves. If we don't keep control of our governments, or of people we give authority over us, then we become puppets. I think I'd take a risk, maybe even a major one, if I felt I was in personal danger of having that happen.

Jose and Miriam Arguelles, in *Mandala*, write, "Since it is the mind of man that realizes and integrates the various parts of a given system, such a system may also be described as a map of consciousness. Consciousness is the power of an organism to order, integrate and transform itself." The students whose work appears in this book, and the hundreds of students whose work does not, testify over and over again that they have grown to a new consciousness as they develop their own individual powers to order, integrate, and transform themselves. They are making connections.

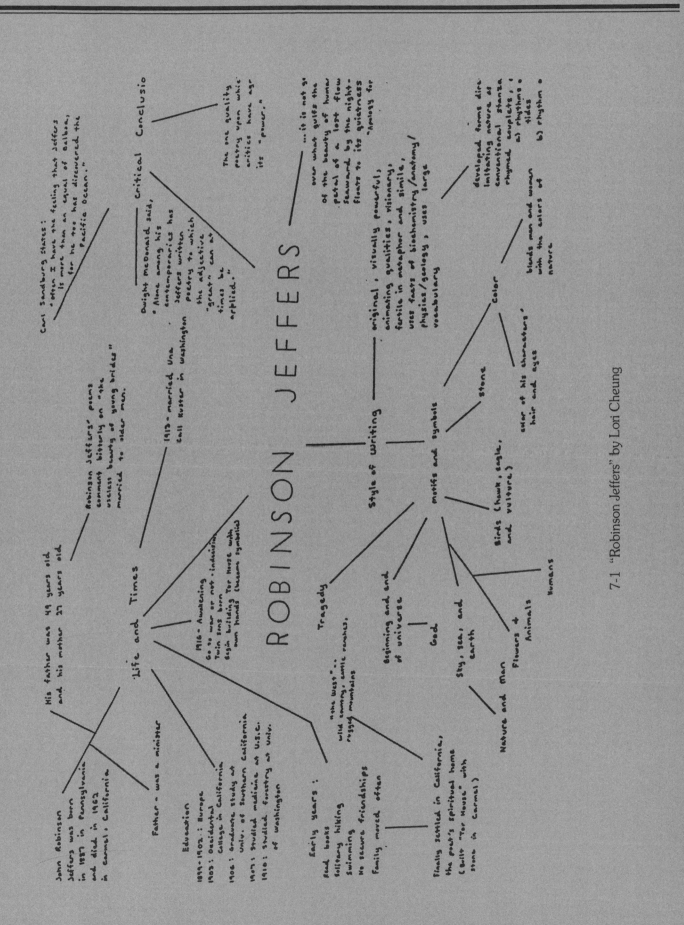

7-1 "Robinson Jeffers" by Lori Cheung

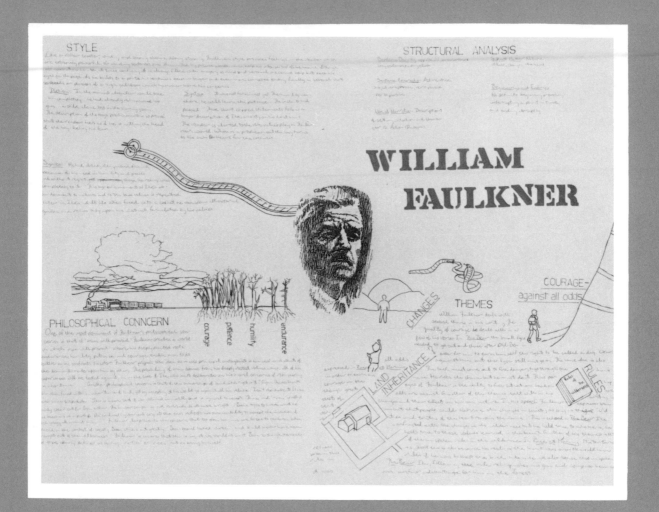

7-2   "Faulkner" by Gretchen Anderson, Billy Tsai,
and Gretchen Skillman

7-3 "Kenneth Patchen" by Mimi Nicosia

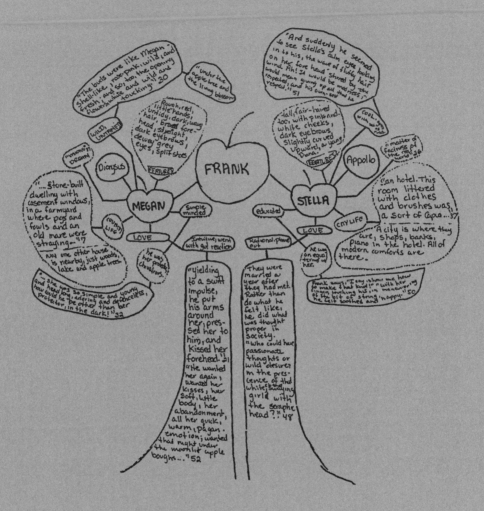

7-4 *The Apple Tree* by Michelle Mebine

7-5 The Breakdown in Order in *Lord of the Flies*
by Sandy Brophy

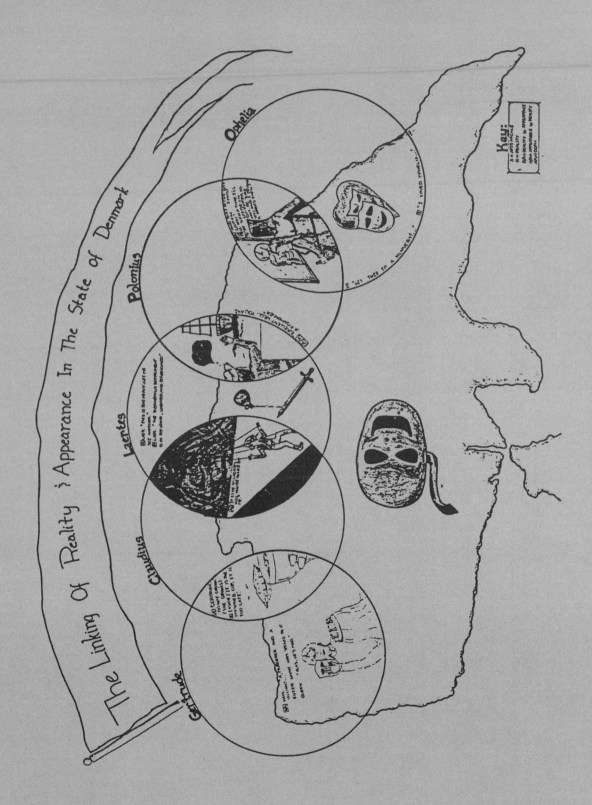

7-6 Reality vs. Illusion in *Hamlet* by Mike Egan and Doug Alexander

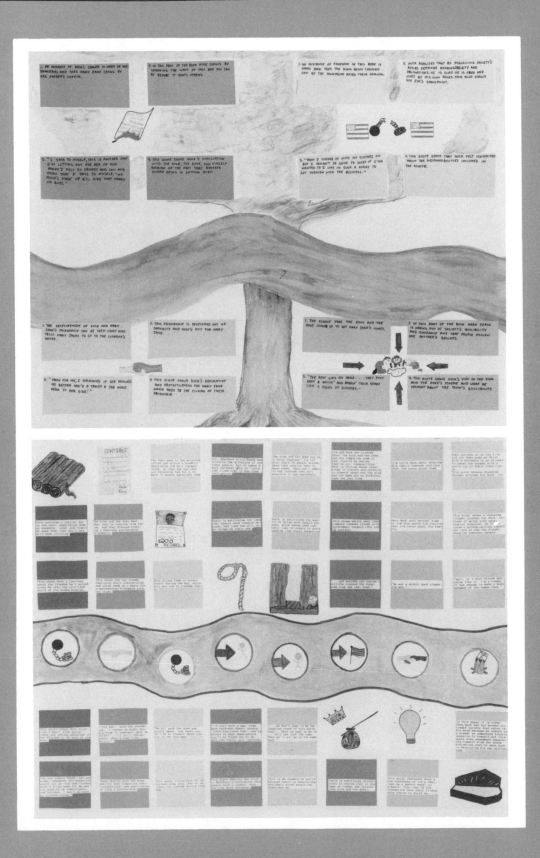

7-7   Huck Finn Chapter Map

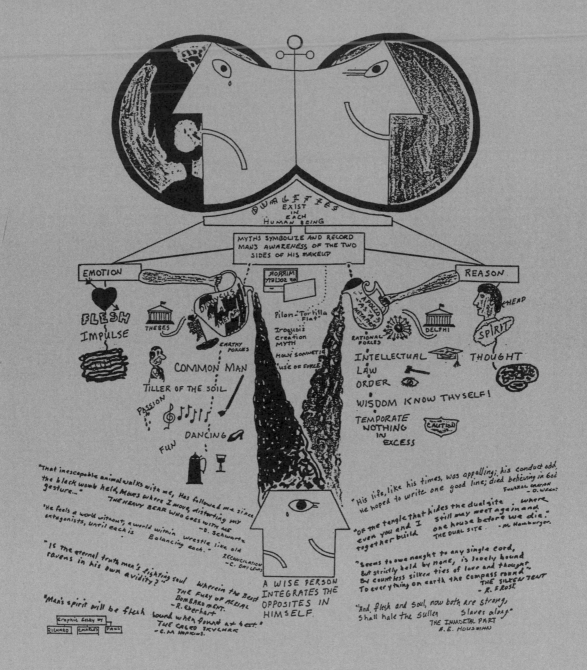

7-8 "Dualities" by Richard Paul

7-9 Civil Disobedience Mandala by Sarah Blake and Sharon McGregor

"Teiresias" by Barry Tribuzio

AFTERWORD

BALANCING THE CURRICULUM

That which is always beginning , over and over.

WALLACE STEVENS

*For last year's words belong to last year's
   language
And next year's words await another voice.*

T. S. ELIOT, *FOUR QUARTETS*

There are many ways to work toward balancing the curriculum. We visualize (although neither of us can draw it) a circle of teeter-totters, all with a central fulcrum, but moving at various rates of speed. If this teeter-totter mandala were perfectly balanced, it would be still, all boards straight out from the center, neither up nor down. The stasis of uniformity is not our goal, however: our teaching focuses on *balancing* rather than *balance*. In our view of the teeter-totter classroom, the center would be the still point, while the boards would move at their own rates, in their own trajectories, creating the harmony that comes only from diversity.

The teacher's stance: Janus, looking back, looking forward, from the imbalance that is always moving toward balance; from Stevens' paradise that "lies in flawed words and stubborn sounds" to Eliot's "still point of the turning world." Perpetually unprepared for the new faces that we meet in September, we spend our summers designing the perfect curriculum for the students who just left us. Yet the urge is always toward that elusive goal—student, teacher, text—in perfect equilibrium.

Knowing that whatever we design in July will have to be revised in September, we focus on balancing the four functions—observe, analyze, imagine, feel. We keep one eye on the poem. We keep the other on the student. But there is not just one student, or one poem for each kind of student. Or one teacher. And here the metaphor mutates, leaving us with, not Janus, but Argus, whose thousand teacher eyes end up in the prescience of the peacock's plume.

This thousand-eyed vision becomes its own map of consciousness. A growing network of teachers underscore Stevens' image of "a thousand people on one string," as we share our ideas of how to enhance the colloquy of the classroom—those vital collaborations and conversations that underlie the making of new metaphors, new visions.

We hope that you will use these ideas as metaphors for your own adaptations of mandalas and maps as you develop new ways of helping students think around the mandala of the four functions and develop whatever patterns emerge. Both of us would be extremely pleased to have you share your ideas about using graphics with us. We leave you, then, to draw your own conclusions, we hope both literally and figuratively.